JENNY JONES

What A Light You Are

This novel is entirely a work of fiction. The names, characters and incidents portrayed in it are the work of the author's imagination. Any resemblance to actual persons, living or dead, events or localities is entirely coincidental.

First edition

Cover art by May Taylor

This book was professionally typeset on Reedsy.
Find out more at reedsy.com

To J.R., you are and forever will be the spark that started it all.

Contents

Playlist

2 Most Wanted x Beyonce, Miley Cyrus
Beautiful Things x Benson Boone
Running Up That Hill x Kate Bush
Unwritten x Natasha Bedingfield
Night Changes x One Direction
Selfish x Justin Timberlake
Smash into You x Beyonce
Unthinkable x Alicia Keys
Dreams x Fleetwood Mac
Willow x Taylor Swift
Lover x Taylor Swift
Bloom x Aqyila

Zodiac Signs

Wren - Sagittarius

William - Taurus

Dove - Aquarius

Lark - Scorpio

Raven - Virgo

Ayla -Pisces

Eric - Cancer

Marcus -Gemini

One

Birthday Girl

Wren

December 21st

Did this asshole just grab my ass?

I spin around in disbelief, locking eyes with the suspect. Of course, he looks like he has a frat house sexual assault charge or two under his belt. He's show-muscular, pale, with a sharp nose and a devilish smirk. Thin, straight blonde hair brushes his broad shoulders, and his icy blue eyes are devoid of remorse. Is Twilight casting?

He grins as if expecting me to thank him for the unsolicited grope. I don't understand men like him—bold, arrogant, the kind who think women will curtsy to their faux confidence. I return his grin, tilting my head with a "come here" gesture. He leans in, probably expecting some coquettish whisper.

As his face nears mine, I shift slightly to the right as if aiming for his ear. His smirk widens. I lick my bottom lip, savoring what's about to happen. My left fist flies into his jaw, hard. Pain shoots down my hand as pins and needles explode across my fingers, but the sight of Blondie stumbling back in shock is worth it. His doppelgänger friend catches him, both of them mirroring identical expressions of outrage. I might not have done much damage to his trust-fund face, but I've bruised his ego, and that's enough for me.

I shake out my hand like they do in the movies, though it does little to dull the sharp ache radiating from my knuckles. I punched exactly as I was taught in college self-defense classes—feet planted, twist at the hips, elbow bent. The fact that my hand isn't broken feels like a small victory. I blow Blondie a kiss, grinning. I'm not a violent person, but keeping your hands to yourself is a lesson worth teaching.

"I can't believe we just got kicked out of the club on your birthday," Lark mutters as we round the corner from the bar.

"Well, when you start a fight, it's kind of inevitable," Raven replies, wobbling slightly in the too-small heels she borrowed from me. She winces as she tries to adjust her feet, muttering about her poor decision-making.

After security reached the dance floor, they took one look at the scene and promptly threw us out. Apparently, groping isn't an offense, but punching someone is. I didn't mind. The club's watered-down drinks, sweaty under-25 crowd, and overplayed radio hits were draining my birthday spirit anyway.

"Let's be real, I'll start a fight every single night an asshole thinks it's okay to grab my ass," I declare, my voice echoing with defiance.

"To be fair, that punch was impressive, Wren!" Raven says proudly, giving my shoulder a playful nudge.

"Very cute," Dove interjects, her voice muffled by the coat she has pulled up over her ears and nose. "Now, can we grab food at that diner we passed earlier? I'm freezing."

Dove claims she's too old for clubs but still tags along, playing designated driver and occasional dance partner. The temperature hovers near 20 degrees, but since it's my birthday, we're braving the cold, cheap shoes, and fast-fashion dresses. You only turn 28 once, after all.

We turn onto Carlyle Avenue, Dove leading the way. Spotting the bulky silver diner at the block's end, we quicken our pace. The air tonight is merciless, biting at any exposed skin. It's not easy being a winter baby.

The diner's warmth envelops us as we step inside, the jingle of the bell above the door announcing our arrival. Despite the clunky interior— four red booths, a polished counter lined with weathered stools—the space radiates charm. The smell of coffee and fried food fills the air, and a dessert display near the entrance tempts with cakes and pies. My gaze locks onto a strawberry shortcake that looks almost too good to be real.

"Take a seat wherever you'd like," the waitress calls from behind the counter. Lark darts ahead, claiming the corner booth. We follow, shedding coats and sighing in relief as we sink into the cracked faux-leather seats. Across from us stands a jukebox, its scratched surface hinting at decades of service. I cross the aisle to inspect the song selection—Fleetwood Mac, Mary J. Blige, Natasha Bedingfield, even Nicki Minaj.

The waitress approaches, her tired smile still genuine. "What can I get you ladies to drink?"

"Four Shirley Temples, please," I say with a mischievous grin. My sisters exchange knowing looks. Shirley Temples are our go-to for sneaky fun. As the waitress jots down our order, I spot her eyes flicker with curiosity but she says nothing. Lark orders our burgers—two regular, one plain, and one cheeseburger with extra mustard, knowing everyone's preferences.

As the waitress heads off, Raven leans in. "That punch might be the highlight of your 28th birthday, Wren."

I smirk. "It was definitely a moment."

A few minutes later, the jukebox hums to life as Fleetwood Mac's "Dreams" fills the diner. The familiar tune draws us into an impromptu dance session, swaying and spinning in our little corner, our laughter blending with the music. For a brief moment, the night feels magical again.

As we settle back into the booth, I catch sight of a man at the counter. He's stunning—broad-shouldered, dressed in a wine-colored sweater over a crisp white shirt. His presence is magnetic, but something about him feels familiar, almost hauntingly so. He leans towards the brunette beside him, their interaction easy and intimate. My heart sinks. He's taken.

I sigh, letting the fantasy drift away as I pour tequila from my hidden stash into our Shirley Temples. As the night winds down, I take one last glance at the man as he pays his bill. For a moment, our eyes meet. There's something unspoken, a connection I can't explain. But then he's gone, the bell above the door jingling softly as he leaves.

I take a bite of my burger, leaning back into the booth. The night may not have gone as planned, but surrounded by my sisters, I know it was still worth celebrating.

* * *

William

Ayla's text had piqued my curiosity, though I already had a feeling about its purpose. Still, I played along and agreed to meet her for a late dinner at the diner she swore had "the best shakes." Personally, I found the shakes decent at best—hardly deserving of such high praise. Words have meanings, after all.

I arrived promptly at 10 p.m., as instructed, and ordered a burger, regrettably so. To salvage the meal, I treated myself to a slice of cheesecake, which proved to be a much better decision. By the time Ayla finally breezed in, half an hour late, I was already halfway through the dessert.

"Hey! Oh my god, traffic. Sorry," she exclaimed, rushing over to the counter with all the energy of someone who didn't just waste my time.

"Yeah," I replied dryly, unable to mask my irritation.

"Oh, come on," she teased, rolling her eyes in a way that instantly transported me back to our childhood. She was 24 now, no longer the carefree kid I remembered, though she still had her moments.

"How's school going, Ay?" I asked, knowing full well she'd dodge the question.

"How's work going, Will?" she shot back with a cheeky grin, the perfect uno reverse.

"Work is grand. How is school, Ay?" I pressed. Her smile faltered, and she fixed me with a flat stare.

"School is fine, William. Is that hot guy still at your office?" she asked, pivoting to her favorite pastime—testing my patience as her older brother. I ignored her question, taking another deliberate bite of cheesecake.

"Oh yeah, Erin!" she exclaimed, feigning a dramatic wipe of her brow. "How is he? Is he married yet?" Her batting lashes and mischievous smirk were designed to bait me, but I refused to rise to it.

As she finally slid into her seat, the bell above the door chimed, drawing my attention. I turned instinctively—and froze. She stepped into the diner like a burst of sunlight, her golden skin glowing under the fluorescent lights. Her high cheekbones framed mesmerizing dark green eyes, and her smile was so genuine it seemed to light up the room. She was stunning, but it wasn't just her beauty that struck me—it was her presence, magnetic and undeniable, as if the air itself shifted to accommodate her.

"Will?" Ayla's voice snapped me back to reality. She tilted her head, her confusion evident.

I shook off the spell and turned back to my sister, clearing my throat. "What's going on, Ayla?"

Her expression softened, and she leaned forward conspiratorially. "I know mom and dad aren't getting along right now, and I know it's rough for you too. But I have a plan to fix it."

I sighed, turning back to my plate as I took another bite of cheesecake. "They're adults, Ay. They live in the same house. What are we supposed to do?"

Ayla leaned forward, undeterred. "Sometimes love just needs a little push! Therapy is a good start," she declared, as though she hadn't just suggested the family equivalent of a rom-com parent trap.

I remained skeptical, but her determination was contagious. Eventually, I agreed to reach out to Dad while she spoke to Mom. Ayla animatedly laid out her plan, her voice full of excitement, but my mind kept drifting back to the woman who had walked in moments earlier.

She was dancing now, her red dress swaying with each graceful movement. There was something carefree and joyous about her, a lightness that seemed to transcend the mundane atmosphere of the diner. It was mesmerizing. She exuded an effortless charm, radiating a joy that felt infectious and inviting. For a brief moment, I wished I could join her, cast aside the weight of the world, and lose myself in the music, if only for a fleeting moment.

"Will?" Ayla's voice brought me back again. She was leaning over my plate, sniffing at the cheesecake.

"You can have it," I offered, sliding the plate toward her.

"Oh no, I just wanted to smell it," she replied, fiddling with the rolled utensils in front of her. I gave her a skeptical look, the corner of my mouth quirking upward in amusement.

"Ayla, eat the damn cake," I said with a sigh.

"Alright, Ike," she quipped, giggling as she took a bite. I smirked at her quick comeback, shaking my head.

As she detailed the finer points of her plan, I found my thoughts wandering once more to the woman in red. Now seated across the room, her presence still glowed, though I noticed something deeper beneath her radiant exterior—a hint of sadness, perhaps? A trace of something unresolved.

Acting on impulse, I flagged down our waitress as she passed by. "Could I get the bill, please?" I asked, and then, lowering my voice, added, "And could you do me a small favor?"

The waitress returned moments later with a notepad and pen. Quickly, I scribbled a note, folded it neatly, and handed it back to her along with a $50 bill as a tip. As she walked away, I glanced at the woman one last time. My chest tightened with a strange sense of urgency, a quiet voice whispering that this wasn't the end of our story. But for now, I rejoined the moment with Ayla, ready to face whatever her wild plan had in store.

Two

Alignment

Wren

December 30th

Standing behind the large granite counter at Dove's cozy bakery, surrounded by the aroma of freshly baked treats, I rang up orders while customers eagerly claimed their goodies. In my hand, I absently twirled a note—the one that had mysteriously appeared on my birthday at the diner. Its sender remained a mystery. The waitress who passed it to me had been frustratingly tight-lipped, claiming she'd been paid well to keep their identity a secret.

The note's simple message, *"What a light you are,"* had felt thrilling at first but grew more cryptic with time. No name, no contact information—just those five words. It left me in a strange place, feeling both seen and unsettled.

"Hey, you can head out now. Polly's coming in soon," Dove's melodious voice broke through my thoughts.

"Thanks, Dovey. I finished setting up the Valentine's Day display, so you're all set." I untied my apron and shook out my curls, loose tendrils bouncing around my shoulders. Dove, dressed in her usual soft creams and whites, radiated calm. Her cardigan draped gracefully over her slender frame, mirroring the serenity she carried in everything she did. She glanced up from tidying the tables, her eyes soft but curious.

"I know you're working on your business, Wren," she began gently, "but have you thought about taking on clients outside the family?"

I paused, smoothing my coat collar as I processed the question. "I don't think I'm ready yet," I admitted, my voice betraying a hint of doubt. My dream of building an interior design and event planning business was deeply personal. It wasn't just a job—it was *me*. The idea of failing at it paralyzed me.

Dove nodded, her understanding expression a balm to my nerves. "You'll know when the time is right," she said softly.

"Love you," I called as I stepped out into the crisp winter air, the scent of the bakery clinging to my coat.

The city bustled around me, a soothing hum of life as I made my way down the street. My attention was caught by the glimmer of a Christmas tree through the tall glass walls of a sleek, unmarked building. The towering tree, adorned with shimmering ribbons and twinkling lights, filled me with a familiar spark of creativity and nostalgia.

Curious, I stepped inside. The lobby was immaculate, all polished slate-gray surfaces and modern elegance. Two impeccably dressed security guards sat behind a massive desk, their crisp uniforms adding to the sophistication of the space.

"Wow, that tree is incredible," I remarked, my gaze lingering on the masterpiece. "Do you know who decorated it? I'd love to work with them."

The guards exchanged brief glances before looking over my shoulder.

"So, you're a decorator?" A smooth, deep voice spoke from behind me, sending a shiver down my spine. I turned to find a tall man in a flawlessly tailored gray suit. His tousled hair gave him a casual yet polished air, and his piercing gaze held mine as a mischievous grin spread across his face.

"Yes," I said, nodding. "I'm a decorator. Wren Reese. My pleasure." I extended my hand, forcing a confident smile despite the flutter of nerves in my chest.

"Eric Pearson," he replied, taking my hand in a firm, lingering hand-shake. "The pleasure is all mine." His dimpled smile was disarming, his magnetic presence both captivating and unnerving.

"Are you looking for decorating services?" I asked, slipping into my professional tone. His smirk deepened, his expression unreadable but undeniably charming.

"I most certainly am," he replied. "Our previous contractor… let's just say reliability was an issue. We're looking for someone dependable."

His words struck a nerve. Outside my family, "flake" and "fickle" had been thrown my way far too often. I straightened my posture, determined to push past the self-doubt creeping in.

As we discussed his office's decorating needs, I felt a spark of excitement reignite within me. When the guards handed me a pad and pen, I jotted down my email address. Mental note: *Invest in business cards ASAP.*

Eric unfolded the note, his amused smirk widening. "'Littlebird95?'" he asked, barely suppressing a chuckle.

I rolled my eyes playfully. "High school email. I'm working on a business one," I explained. "I haven't finalized a name yet. I'm torn between two—one feels perfect, but the other is more practical."

His gaze sharpened with curiosity. "Go with your heart," he said simply, his confidence in the advice as unshakable as the man himself.

His words hit me harder than expected. When did I become so afraid to trust myself? I used to be bold, decisive—*fearless.* Approaching 30, that boldness had dulled, replaced by the weight of responsibilities and the fear of failure. But his matter-of-fact statement reminded me of the person I once was—and the person I wanted to be again.

With a warm smile and a casual farewell, Eric strode off, leaving me with a strange mixture of hope and doubt.

Back on the street, the cold air stung my cheeks as I mulled over the encounter. Would he really reach out? Or was his interest in *me* rather than my work? I hadn't even shown him my portfolio—what if he thought I was a scam artist?

Still, the interaction had sparked something important: clarity. I needed to act, to start putting the pieces of my dream together.

To-do list:

- Establish a professional email address.
- Build a portfolio.
- Order business cards.
- Decide on a business name.

With every step, my confidence grew. I wasn't about to let "30" or fear of failure hold me back. I was capable. I was talented. And I could do this.

Head held high, cheeks flushed from the cold, I strode down the busy block, determination burning brighter than ever.

* * *

Riding the train home, my mind was alight with fireworks of creativity as I brainstormed potential business names. Each idea seemed fleeting, none quite sticking until, as if struck by lightning, it came to me: *Nest Designs.* The name rolled off my tongue effortlessly, a nod to my parents' bird-themed love story. It felt personal yet professional, though I wondered if it leaned too much into the bird motif. Still, I couldn't deny how right it felt.

As the train came to a halt, I stepped out, greeted by the unwelcome scent of urine mingled with coffee and wet dog. Pulling my coat up over my nose, I navigated the familiar blue and gray stairs toward the Miller Street exit. Grateful that the station was only two blocks from home, I set off, relieved that the day had spared me the misery of snowfall.

The walk gave me time to reflect on the weight of living at home again. At 28, it wasn't where I imagined I'd be. The harsh economy had forced me to retreat to my childhood sanctuary, unable to afford rent as a "recent" graduate. Memories of my cozy uptown apartment with Josh drifted into my mind, bittersweet and laced with longing.

When we split, he kept the apartment. I hadn't been able to contribute to the rent anyway. Losing not just the relationship but also the space I'd lovingly curated felt like a deeper wound. That apartment had been my sanctuary, filled with pieces of my heart in every corner—carefully chosen decor that exuded warmth and style. Josh's contributions? Takeout boxes and his prized Ravens jersey, proudly displayed in the bedroom.

Our relationship hadn't been a stormy one. It was a quiet erosion, a slow unraveling of connection. In college, we'd laughed, shared dreams, and built inside jokes. But post-graduation life drained him into a corporate drone, and the spark we once shared dimmed. By the time we ended things last spring, it already felt like a lifetime ago.

Determined not to dwell on the past, I focused on small joys, like the movie night I'd planned with my sisters. I pulled out my phone and sent a quick message in the group chat.

Almost immediately, two thumbs-up emojis popped up—Raven was on her way, and Lark was likely already nestled in the basement. Dove would probably arrive soon with bakery treats in tow.

I kicked off my shoes, hung my coat and scarf, and glanced toward the living room. The warm flicker of the fireplace hinted at one of my parents' romantic evenings. Decades into their marriage, they still had date nights three times a week, infusing their lives with a spark that most couples lost long before. Watching them, I couldn't help but feel a twinge of longing for something similar—real, genuine, enduring love.

Heading to the kitchen, I grabbed a couple of water bottles and tossed a bag of popcorn into the microwave. The sound of footsteps coming up from the basement made me turn just in time to see Lark, wrapped in her favorite orange blanket.

"What's going on?" she asked, her concern evident.

"Just getting snacks ready for movie night," I replied casually.

She raised an eyebrow. "Come on, Wren. Movie night always means you've got something on your mind."

I sighed, pulling the popcorn from the microwave and swapping it for butter. "It's just been one of those days," I admitted.

Her expression softened, and she came to stand beside me. "I'm here whenever you're ready to talk," she said, her voice gentle. She snagged a handful of popcorn and kissed my cheek before heading back downstairs, her presence a comforting reminder that I wasn't alone.

The doorbell rang, followed by the creak of the front door. I didn't need to look to know Raven had arrived.

"Hey, you filthy whore," I called out with a smirk, spotting her at the kitchen entrance. She stood there in her work pantsuit, hair escaping its tight bun, holding two tall bottles of tequila with a grin that screamed mischief.

"Well, if the shoe fits, slore," she shot back, finishing our inside joke as I walked over to relieve her of the tequila. I kissed her cheek, earning a dramatic grimace.

Despite her petite frame, Raven carried a ferocity that had earned her the nickname "Pit Bull" in high school. She was fiercely protective, her strength and loyalty unmatched. As the second oldest, she often took on the "dad" role in our dynamic, balancing Dove's nurturing "mom" energy.

Raven discarded her blazer onto a stool before heading downstairs. Seconds later, I heard Lark's delighted scream, followed by an unmistakable "Ouch!"—no doubt a jab to the ribs for trying to climb Raven like she used to as a kid.

Dove's headlights glowed through the living room curtains, signaling her arrival. Grabbing the popcorn and water bottles, I followed the sound of music and clinking shot glasses down to the basement, where the real party was just beginning. The worries of the day melted away as laughter, warmth, and the unshakable bond of sisterhood wrapped around me.

Three

Coffee Runs

William

January 3rd

"Dad, are you really keeping your poker face on for this one?" I asked, my fingers tapping rhythmically on my keyboard. The office was unusually quiet, a welcome change after the chaos of the holidays. Silence had its allure.

"Son, we're in our 60s. Your mother is having a midlife crisis, and she'll snap out of it," my dad's gruff voice crackled through the phone.

"I don't think wanting to explore and travel qualifies as a midlife crisis. And she wants to do it *with you,* might I add," I replied, closing my spreadsheet with a frustrated sigh.

"Travel? Out of the house? We finally have the mortgage paid off. We're both retired. What's wrong with exploring the new movies on the Netflix you set up for us?" His stubbornness was as familiar as it was exasperating.

"Okay, Dad. I've done my part, but when Mom's in Italy living her best life, don't say I didn't try to help." I shut my laptop, leaning back in my chair.

My stepdad—my *dad*—was once so full of life. When he met my mom, he was a kindergarten teacher, my kindergarten teacher, in fact. Even as a kid, I'd noticed the way they looked at each other. By the time I moved on to the next grade, he was joining us for Sunday dinners. Soon, he never left. Over time, he moved on to teaching third grade, a job he said was easier on his back, but he never lost his humor or his knack for wild plans.

That man seemed long gone. Now he'd settled into a sedentary existence, while my mom radiated energy and a passion for life. She'd worked as a secretary at City Hall before retiring, and now she wanted Dad to rediscover life alongside her. She suspected he was depressed and had urged him to consider counseling, but he refused to budge.

"She's not going anywhere, Will. I know your mother," Dad said firmly, his words resolute but tinged with emotion.

"I'll leave you to it, then," I said, cutting the conversation short. Hanging up, I grabbed my coat and headed for the elevator, restless with the weight of their situation.

On my way out, I called over to Shiva, my voice echoing in the quiet office. "Hey, Shiva, I'm stepping out for coffee. Let me know if anything comes through for the Harrison-Peters file."

Shiva, absorbed in her phone call, gave me a thumbs-up and a quick nod, her Bluetooth headset blending seamlessly into her dark hair.

The coffee shop buzzed with activity, the aroma of fresh brews mingling with the chatter of patrons. I joined the back of the line, the hum of conversation blending with soft background music. Ordering a simple black coffee with oat milk and sugar, I swiped my card and let my gaze wander across the room.

Most people were glued to their phones, their faces bathed in the cold glow of their screens. The disconnect was palpable, a stark reminder of how much technology dominated our lives. Then, amidst the crowd, I noticed *her.*

She stood out like a vivid brushstroke on a gray scale canvas. The dancing girl from the diner.

Her effortless style drew my attention—black leggings, combat boots, and a lilac coat that sparkled faintly under the café lights, draped over her shoulders like a soft cloud. She tapped on her phone with casual grace, her presence radiating a quiet intensity. The mystery of her ethnic background, the elegance in her stance—it all added to the allure, leaving me captivated. I barely registered the cashier clearing her throat until I moved forward with a tight smile to grab my receipt.

Leaning against the back wall near the pick-up counter, I sipped my coffee and let my eyes wander again. The café bustled with life, yet my focus kept circling back to her. She was deep in thought, her gaze distant, as if lost in her own world. I wanted to approach her, to end this strange dance of fate, but interrupting her in the crowded café felt… intrusive.

My name cut through my thoughts, called out by an exasperated barista. Jolted, I stepped forward to retrieve my drink, my phone buzzing just as it touched my hand. The screen lit up with Shiva's name.

"William, have you checked your email?" she asked, her voice tinged with urgency.

"No, why?" I replied, already bracing myself.

"There's been a change to the Harrison file," she said, her words sharp and deliberate.

"The Harrison-Peters file?" I asked, my stomach sinking.

"That's the change… sir," she confirmed, her tone making the implications clear.

"What?" I exclaimed, abandoning my coffee on the cluttered counter. My heart raced as I pushed through the crowd, heading for the back exit. The air outside hit me like a slap, sharp and bracing, but it did little to clear the storm of questions swirling in my mind.

* * *

Wren

I'm walking the four blocks from Dove's bakery to Century Café, the only place in Merritt City that makes a caramel latte exactly the way I like it. The shop is small, always packed, and inconvenient, but caffeine is a cruel master.

I hate that Dove's bakery is smack in the middle of the business district. Sure, the exposure is great, but it's an endless sea of suits—each person looking more miserable than the last. People-watching is my guilty pleasure, though. I love assigning strangers lives, names, and maybe even pets. Anything to liven up the monotony.

As I near Century Café, my steps falter. There he is: *Mystery Hottie.* He's holding the door open for two women leaving the shop, his face unreadable, his suit as blandly expensive as the rest of the men in this part of town. I want to write him off as just another soulless corporate drone, but something stops me. There's a depth about him that intrigues me. It's like there's a story beneath the polished exterior, and I find myself wanting to uncover it.

My pace quickens. I don't want to miss this chance to figure him out, but then I remember the brunette he was with at the diner. My steps slow. He's intriguing, yes, but not enough to go down the road of potential home-wrecking. I pull out my phone, opening the group chat with my sisters to distract myself.

Wren: Mystery Hunk is @ Century
Raven: What should I do with this info, Wren??
Wren: Can someone remove Raven from the chat?

Lark: Get his number!!
Dove: Who?
Raven: Don't bother that man.
Lark: Ray, SHHH!

Pushing open the door of the café, I'm immediately enveloped by the rich aroma of freshly brewed coffee. The shop is cozy, with warm hardwood floors and a mix of mismatched chairs and couches in soft, inviting hues. Sage-green walls are adorned with planters suspended from the ceiling in vibrant blue pots, giving the space a refreshing, lively energy. It's the kind of spot that feels like a small escape from the dull gray of the business district—a perfect place to recharge.

The line is long, as always. I pull out my phone to kill time, diving into the group chat as I inch forward. My sisters are deep into a playful thread about Dove's recent encounter with a doctor who had come into the bakery craving two dozen bear claws. The donut jokes and memes come fast, making me bite my lip to keep from laughing out loud.

Dove, at 32, has been through her share of ups and downs in the love department. She married her high school sweetheart at 18, thinking they'd make it forever. But after seven years, they split. It wasn't a dramatic divorce—just the quiet realization that they'd grown apart. They're still friends, shockingly enough, and Dove even has an invite to his upcoming wedding. Go figure.

Since then, she's focused on her bakery. Sure, she dates now and then, but nothing serious. Lark thinks she's too picky, but I understand. Getting burned once makes you cautious. Dove's marriage ending wasn't just the loss of a relationship; it shattered the fairy-tale image of what she thought love was supposed to be.

The monotony of the line breaks as the barista calls out a name for the third time: "William." My head instinctively turns, and there he is—*Mystery Hottie.*

I freeze as he steps forward to claim his drink, the shock of recognition washing over me. It's him. The man from the diner on my birthday. *William.*

From this close, he's even more striking. Confidence radiates off him, magnetic and intoxicating. His smooth brown skin, like rich chocolate, catches the light, while his tailored black suit fits him like a second skin. The subtle contrast of a light gray shirt underneath only enhances his polished look. His broad shoulders exude strength, but the glasses perched on his face add a touch of humanity to his god-like aura.

Why is he here? Is this mere coincidence, or is something else at play? My mind races as he takes his drink with a quiet determination. I want to say something, to bridge this strange connection that seems to keep pulling us together, but the moment slips through my fingers as he walks toward the door.

I watch him leave, his presence lingering like a ripple in the air. The barista calls my name, snapping me back to reality. I collect my latte and return to the group chat, where my sisters have moved on to planning Dove's birthday. The ordinary rhythm of life reclaims me, but a part of my mind stays fixed on the mystery of William.

Four

Beginnings

Wren

January 15th

Lark crashes onto my bed, sending my laptop tumbling to the side. I'm in the middle of creating yet another email address, hoping to snag a fresh two-month trial of Netflix. My grand business plans are still firmly in the realm of imagination, and every penny saved counts.

"What are you dooooing?" Lark drawls, sprawling across my bed like she owns the place.

"Making another email," I mutter, nudging her with my foot as I burrow deeper into my cocoon of blankets, silently begging for personal space.

"Stop!" she yells dramatically, striking a pose like she's about to deliver the idea of the century.

I glance up, immediately wary. "Why are you making that face?"

"I saw Dove's new boo… and…" She trails off, shooting me a sly look before climbing upright, her theatrics at full throttle.

Intrigued despite myself, I set the laptop aside and lean in. "And?" I prompt, bracing for the inevitable over-the-top reveal.

Tossing a stray lock of hair behind her ear, she finally exclaims, "Unbelievable!"

"In what way? Oh my god, Lark, just *tell* me," I groan, tossing a pillow at her in mock frustration.

"He's a GINGER!" she announces, eyes wide with faux shock. "A sexy ginger, mind you."

"Wait—are we talking about the doctor who ordered two dozen bear claws?" I ask, raising an eyebrow. "Not groundbreaking, but okay. Is there more, or…?"

Lark leans in conspiratorially. "He's not just any doctor; he's an orthopedic surgeon," she squeals, her Grey's Anatomy obsession seeping into every syllable. Flopping back onto the bed, she grins like a kid who just found the candy stash.

I process this new tidbit, my interest piqued. "How do you know he's a surgeon? Wait, you *saw* him?"

"Yesterday! I caught him sneaking out of the bakery," she says, her grin widening.

"Dove froze like a deer in headlights and claimed he was sampling cakes for his brother's wedding. But get this—he left his work ID on the frosting table. I *might* have peeked."

"Dove hasn't said a word about a wedding. If there *was* one, she'd have recruited the whole family by now. Suspicious." I smirk, watching Lark revel in her detective work. "Impressive sleuthing, soldier."

"Oh, and here's the kicker," Lark adds, sitting up with a mischievous glint in her eye. "The bakery smelled like… I don't know, erotica?"

"Erotica?" I snort. "Dove? In her bakery? During business hours? No way. She wouldn't risk unlocked doors. Someone could've walked in!"

"Maybe not," Lark concedes, giggling as she kicks her feet. "But she's definitely hiding something."

While Lark revels in her theories, I mull over the idea of Dove sneaking in a daytime rendezvous. It feels wildly out of character for her— reserved and cautious as she is—but stranger things have happened. Whatever it is, she'll share when she's ready.

Our gossip session is interrupted by a loud email alert. Lark slides down my legs, replaced quickly by my laptop. With a mix of curiosity and trepidation, I open the email app. The subject line makes my breath hitch: *"Office Decorator Offer Letter."*

I stare at the screen, my mind racing. "I just got offered a job…" I whisper, turning the laptop toward Lark and nudging her to look.

As I skim through the details, my disbelief grows. The salary is double what I've ever earned. Double. On top of that, it's hybrid—remote work with occasional on-site responsibilities—and there's a 3% bonus after the annual review. It's not just a job; it's an opportunity, one that aligns perfectly with my goals.

"This is huge," Lark says, sitting up straighter. Her excitement mirrors the emotions flooding through me—relief, validation, a spark of confidence I haven't felt in a long time.

For a moment, the self-doubt that's haunted me threatens to creep in. *Can I do this? Am I ready?* But I shove those thoughts aside. I manifested this by taking a step toward my dream. This isn't just a paycheck; it's a stepping stone. The experience, the connections, the resources—it's all exactly what I need to bring my business plans to life.

Without hesitation, I click "Reply" and type out my response. "I accept your offer." The words feel surreal, but as I hit send, a wave of determination washes over me. This is the first step, and I'm ready for whatever comes next.

* * *

Wren

February 1st

First day of work. I'm so excited I might throw up.

I woke up three hours earlier than necessary, giving myself ample time to freak out, recover, and find my zen. Music blaring from my favorite playlist, I danced around my room, hyping myself up while deciding on the perfect outfit.

I started with a classic choice: a black pencil skirt paired with a white silk blouse with a Bermuda collar. I laid it out on the bed, pacing around the edges to inspect it from every angle. It wasn't speaking to me. Without a second thought, I swiped it onto the floor. Back to the closet.

Next, I pulled out a saffron-yellow mid-length dress with a square neckline. Bold? Yes. But it perfectly complemented my collarbone and exuded the confidence I wanted to bring to my first day. Yellow might be risky, but I'm a decorator, not an accountant. A decorator should come *decorated.*

With my outfit chosen, I got ready. My hair was styled half-up, half-down, my fresh curls shining and bouncy after yesterday's wash day. I felt radiant. Swinging around the stair railing, I made my way to the living room to gather my things. Purse in hand, I checked for essentials: headphones, charger, emergency makeup kit, and rolled-up ballerina flats stashed in a ziplock bag. At the front door, I slipped on my black, four-inch, closed-toe heels. Ugh, I looked perfect.

The glass tower loomed before me, sleek and imposing, as I arrived 25 minutes early. I paused outside, taking a deep breath to steady myself. *I am happy. I am blessed. I am alive.* With renewed confidence, I stepped inside.

The lobby was a marvel. Polished black floors sparkled with what looked like tiny embedded diamonds, catching the light like a constellation beneath my feet. Glass walls framed by gold trim soared upward, the entire space exuding a Gatsby-era opulence.

I approached the security desk, waiting patiently while the guards handled a small crowd of visitors. One guard caught my eye and gave me a quick, "I'll be right with you" smile. I returned it with a polite nod, turning to take in the grand lobby.

The infamous Christmas tree that had been here during my interview was gone, replaced by a grand piano. My admiration for the space was interrupted by a pang of realization—I'd left my purse at the desk. I spun around abruptly, my mind elsewhere, and collided hard into what I thought was a wall. Only it wasn't a wall.

It was a chest. A *firm* chest.

My eyes traveled upward, past broad shoulders and a strong jaw, until they landed on familiar lips. *William.*

Large hands steadied me by the shoulders, and he leaned down, his face so close I could make out every detail. "Are you alright?" he asked, his voice deep and commanding yet smooth, like velvet wrapped in steel.

I nodded, grinning like a fool. It was finally happening—the meet-cute

I'd imagined a thousand times. His hands lingered for a moment before he stepped back, his gaze meeting mine. He nodded in acknowledgment, exhaling sharply, then walked past me toward the elevators without another word. I turned to watch him go, hoping he might glance back. He didn't.

What just happened? The universe had finally aligned, giving me a chance to collide—literally—with William, the mystery man from the diner and the café. And he acted like that? Rude, dismissive, cold. What a letdown.

* * *

Eric invited me out to lunch for my first day. We ended up at a fancy bistro tucked inside the building, a hidden gem I hadn't known existed. He ordered duck while I opted for Cajun pasta, the dish delivering just the right amount of spice to soothe my nerves.

"This is my way of welcoming you to the firm," Eric said with his signature charm, a small smile tugging at the corner of his lips. He spoke about how excited he was to see what I could bring to the table, setting the tone for the expectations ahead. I matched his energy, sharing a few ideas for the Valentine's party, my first major assignment and performance review rolled into one. The stakes felt high, but his easy demeanor made the conversation flow naturally.

Despite his good looks and smooth confidence, there were no sparks for me. I appreciated the gesture and his polite interest, but it was clear to me he had no intentions beyond professionalism. A small part of me had hoped for a harmless office flirtation to add some thrill to the day, but I quickly dismissed the notion. Maybe my hopeless romantic tendencies had conjured up a narrative that didn't exist. Either way, I focused on making a solid impression.

Back at the office, I met Darren and Caroline, the firm's "Floor Managers." Their title sounded impressive, but they appeared to have a lot of free time, evidenced by the two hours they spent lounging in my office.

We'd first crossed paths in the elevator after my lunch with Eric. As Eric exited on the lobby level, I was left alone in the elevator until Darren and Caroline stepped in. By the time the doors closed, I'd already answered at least 21 rapid-fire questions.

Surprisingly, I didn't mind. I've always been one of those rare people who enjoy small talk, and their easygoing energy made the interaction light and enjoyable. Darren had a sharp wit, constantly throwing out quips that had Caroline rolling her eyes and me laughing. Caroline, with her steady, no-nonsense vibe, balanced Darren's humor perfectly. Together, they had the kind of camaraderie that instantly made me feel at ease.

Before I knew it, the three of us were laughing like old friends, and I realized I'd just scored myself some office besties. Darren even offered to help with the Valentine's party setup, while Caroline promised to introduce me to "the good coffee" in the break room—apparently an upgrade from the lukewarm sludge I'd spotted earlier.

By the end of the day, I felt like I'd found my footing. Between lunch with Eric and bonding with Darren and Caroline, the nerves I'd carried that morning had melted away. Sure, the Valentine's party loomed large, but at least now I knew I had some allies in my corner. That, and the Cajun pasta, was enough to call my first day a success.

Five

New Company

William

February 3rd

Navigating the maze of cubicles on the fifth floor, I weave through the office toward Ramon's door. He's the middleman in the tangled Harrison and Peters acquisition, a deal that feels more like an uphill battle with each passing day. Both parties cling to secrecy, redacting their financials to the point of absurdity. Each document I sift through adds another layer of frustration to an already grueling task.

Before I can reach Ramon's office, something—or someone—pulls my attention. Golden brown legs draw my gaze upward, following the curve of her figure. She's engrossed in her task, the black skirt hugging her in ways that make it hard to look away. Her sandy brown curls cascade over her shoulders like a halo, breaking the monotony of this sterile office space. She moves with a lightness, stringing decorations along the walls, and for a moment, the dreary office hums with life.

I linger, watching as she hangs strings of hearts. Her movements are precise but fluid, a dance that feels unintentional. The back of her neck is exposed as her hair shifts, revealing a small tattoo—too blurry from this angle to discern. Questions creep in as I take in the scene. Why is she here? Why is anyone hanging Valentine's Day decorations in this space? We crossed paths briefly in the lobby, but now, seeing her here, in *my* space, is an unexpected—and unwelcome—surprise.

Snapping out of my daze, I push my thoughts aside and press forward to Ramon's office. When I step inside, his smirk greets me like he's been waiting for this moment.

"Great view, huh?" Ramon says, his tone smug.

I keep my expression impassive as I unbutton my jacket and sink into the chair opposite him. "From the fifth floor?" I ask, raising an eyebrow.

Ramon leans back in his chair, gesturing toward the woman still decorating. "No, I'm talking about *Goldie* out there."

"Why is she here?" My tone is cool, masking the irritation bubbling beneath.

"She's the new 'office decorator,'" he replies, air quotes and all.

I blink, stunned. "What the hell is an office decorator?"

Ramon shrugs. "Don't ask me, man. Eric brought her in. Said something about morale or whatever. I'm not complaining—she's a nice change of scenery."

My jaw tightens. "We just agreed to tighten the budget, and someone hired *that*? A decorator?"

"Take it up with Eric," he says, the smirk never leaving his face. "Word is he took her to lunch on her first day. Guess he's staking his claim."

The comment stings, sparking something protective and territorial in me that I have no right to feel. I stand abruptly, my chair scraping against the floor. "Get the Peters team to release the full financial file," I instruct sharply. "I'll handle Eric. And the 'decorator.'"

I leave without waiting for a reply, my steps quick as I make for the elevator. My gaze flickers to the woman as she steps down from her ladder, her hands full of decorations. She moves gracefully but is distracted by the string of cupids tangled around her ankle. Before I can call out, she stumbles. Instinct propels me forward, catching her in my arms before she falls.

Her breath hitches, her eyes wide before a wry smile spreads across her lips. "Well, we've got to stop meeting like this, *William*," she teases, the faintest laugh in her voice.

"You know my name?" I ask, caught off guard by her familiarity.

She doesn't answer directly, instead disentangling herself from my grip with practiced ease. As she gathers her decorations, I notice the label on the bin: *Wren's Q1 Holiday Decorations*. Wren. The name is as fitting as it is intriguing. She moves toward the elevator, and though I consider offering to help with the bin, I stop myself. There's no point. My decision is already made—she has to go.

On the 21st floor, I stride into Eric's opulent office and settle into his leather chair, waiting for him to return. He eventually strolls in, a picture of ease.

"William," he greets, "to what do I owe the pleasure?"

I don't bother with pleasantries. "Why do we have a new hire? And why, of all things, is she a *decorator*?"

Eric shrugs, heading to his bar cart. "The office needed sprucing up. It's a morale booster."

I slam my fist on his desk, my patience fraying. "We just had a board meeting about the budget. Did any of that stick? Or did Daddy summarize it for you?"

He smirks, pouring bourbon into a glass. "I was there, *William*. May I remind you, we're equals. Senior partners, remember?"

"Her role serves no purpose," I argue, the weight of my responsibilities pressing down. "If sense doesn't reach you, I'll take this to the board."

Eric takes a measured sip of his drink, his confidence maddening. "Go ahead. But good luck explaining why morale doesn't matter."

I leave, my resolve hardened. Eric's reckless hire jeopardizes everything I've been working toward. If I let this slide, my credibility—and my position—is at risk. Wren has to go.

Later, as the office empties, I gather my things and head to the elevator. Lost in thought, I nearly don't notice her until I hear a soft laugh. I glance up, spotting Wren. She's in lilac leggings, her hair in a loose bun, the stray curl framing her face impossibly endearing. Her coat hangs open, revealing a crop top that hints at her casual confidence.

She's radiant, completely unaware of my presence. As the elevator descends, the reality of what I must do collides with the quiet ache of what I wish could be. When we reach the lobby, she walks out ahead of me without a glance back, her laughter echoing faintly in the air. I stay rooted to the spot, the weight of my choice heavy on my shoulders.

Tomorrow, I'll terminate her contract. But tonight, her name lingers on my lips. *Wren.*

Six

Fired Up

Wren

February 10th

The group chat buzzes incessantly on my phone, the drama of Raven's reconciliation with her ex, David, dominating the conversation. Their relationship has always been a tempest, and it seems she's steering straight into the storm again. A shiver runs down my spine at the thought of the inevitable fallout. Raven's recent aloofness—while not unusual for the workaholic she is—feels different this time. She missed our last movie night, a sacred tradition even she rarely skips. Something's off.

The digital chatter fades as I glance up to find Eric leaning against my office doorway, a curious expression on his face. His casual posture belies the intent focus in his gaze, as though trying to piece something together.

"Sorry," I offer, locking my phone and setting it face down on the desk. "My sisters sent out a distress signal."

Eric smirks at that, stepping into the room. "Family drama?"

"You could say that." Rising from my white swivel chair, I smile. "Great to see you, Eric. What's on your mind?"

Eric's calm demeanor carries a trace of understanding. "No worries, family's important. I actually stopped by to ask about the heart statue on the ninth floor."

I raise an eyebrow, intrigued. "You like it?"

He nods, slipping his hands into his pockets. "It caught my eye. I was wondering if you could replicate it on my floor before the 14th. With the party coming up, I thought it'd be a nice touch. I don't want to overload your plate, though."

His consideration earns a genuine smile. "Don't worry, I'll make it happen. Honestly, I wasn't sure if the statue was too much, so I'm glad you like it."

Eric's gaze lingers for a moment, subtle yet noticeable, trailing over the details of my dress before meeting my eyes again. His parting comment catches me off guard, leaving a warm flush in its wake. "Nothing about you is too much," he says, his tone light yet loaded, before turning and walking away.

As his presence fades, reality sets in. The extra workload looms, and I make a mental note to beg Lark for help later.

I'm still seated on the edge of my desk when a soft knock on my open office door pulls my attention. Darren and Caroline peek in, their smiles bright and welcoming.

"Lunch?" Darren asks, hopeful. His freckles scatter across his olive skin, adding to his boyish charm.

"I'd love to, but I'm swamped," I admit, sinking back into my chair with a sigh. The weight of deadlines presses heavy on my shoulders.

Darren grins, pulling a bag from behind his back. "Good thing we brought it to you!" Caroline teases, her blue eyes sparkling.

I laugh, motioning them inside. "You two are lifesavers."

As we settle in to eat, the conversation drifts. Eventually, curiosity gets the better of me. "Do you guys know William?"

Darren raises an eyebrow. "Which William?"

"Tall, very tall. Brown skin. Wears glasses sometimes, but I've seen him without. Serious," I describe, a spark of intrigue lighting my expression.

"Oh, *that* William," Darren says knowingly, exchanging a glance with Caroline.

Their silent communication piques my interest. Sitting up straighter, I ask, "What?"

Caroline hesitates before speaking. "William's the youngest Senior Partner here. Mostly handles financial law cases. He's… by the book. Doesn't talk to many people outside his assistant and senior associates."

I exhale sharply. "So, uptight. Another boring suit. At least he's hot to look at," I mutter, half to myself.

Darren shifts uncomfortably, concern flickering in his eyes. "So you must've heard."

"Heard what?" I ask, the edge in my voice sharpening as I catch the pity in his tone.

Caroline answers quietly, as if trying to soften the blow. "William's trying to void your contract. He's meeting with the board in 60 days."

The words hit like a punch. "Wait, what? He's trying to *fire* me? Why?!"

Silence stretches between us. Anger surges, hot and uncontrollable, propelling me to my feet. My chair screeches against the floor as I storm out of the office, blazer forgotten on the back of my chair.

The elevator ride to the twelfth floor feels both endless and too short. My fury intensifies as I stride to William's office, ignoring the curious stares. Without hesitation, I push open his door, startling him mid-call. His eyes narrow as he quickly ends the conversation, adjusting his silver tie with maddening composure.

"What the hell is your problem?" I demand, fists clenched at my sides, my voice shaking with anger.

William's calm demeanor remains intact. "Excuse me?"

"Why are you trying to void my contract?" I press, stepping closer, fire in my gaze.

William rises slowly, his towering frame intimidating but failing to sway me. A fleeting smirk ghosts across his lips before he answers, "It's not personal. Eric hired you irresponsibly. We had a strict budget, and your role… well, it's unnecessary. We're within our rights to terminate before your probation ends."

I blink, stunned by the cold detachment in his words. "Not personal? You're playing with my livelihood, and you call it *business*?"

He shrugs, his tone clipped. "That's exactly what it is—business."

Something in me snaps. Without another word, I spin on my heel and storm out, rage and disbelief warring within me. As I wait for the elevator, the memory of the man from the diner—the mysterious, intriguing stranger—clashes with the corporate automaton I just faced.

The doors close behind me, but the bitter taste of betrayal lingers.

* * *

William

Here's the revised version of your chapter, polished for clarity, flow, and consistency:

My gaze lifts from my desk to find Wren standing in the doorway, her presence a stark contrast to the lightness she usually carries. Today, she's fuming, her anger radiating off her in waves. The intensity of her emotions tugs at something deep within me, stirring instincts I'd rather ignore. Why does her shift in demeanor affect me so much? Pull yourself together, man.

I hastily end the call with my sister, offering some excuse as Wren's voice cuts through the room. She hesitates, as if trying to steady herself before speaking, and then her eyes meet mine. Her gaze is sharp, her emotions laid bare, and it sears through me with disarming intensity.

"What's your problem?" she demands, her words slicing through the air with precision. There's a rawness to her anger, but beneath it lies something else—vulnerability. The sight of her standing there, fists clenched, her breath coming in quick bursts, stirs something primal in me. I hate seeing her this upset, but I can't deny the magnetism of her presence.

Her semi-sheer blouse catches the light, offering glimpses of her form—the subtle curve of her waist, the faint outline of a mole near her ribs. My gaze lingers for a moment too long before I snap myself out of it, dragging my focus back to the matter at hand.

"Excuse me?" I manage, my voice steadier than I feel. Her expression hardens further, the fury in her eyes giving way to a flicker of hurt.

"Why are you trying to void my contract?" she presses, her voice laced with equal parts indignation and wounded pride.

This wasn't how I planned for her to find out. I'd intended to handle it professionally, to sit her down and explain the financial realities behind her position. But office rumors travel faster than intentions, and here we are. I start to explain, outlining the budget constraints and the rationale behind my decision. But she's not interested in my logic. She turns on her heel and storms out, leaving me with a mix of frustration and something I can't quite name.

As her retreating figure disappears down the hall, I find myself conflicted. Part of me is relieved to have the confrontation over with. Another part of me can't help but admire the fire in her, the way she refuses to back down. It's infuriating, and yet… irresistible.

The following day begins as usual. At 5 a.m., I head out for a jog with Jerry Smith, followed by a brisk mile on the treadmill and a crossword puzzle before work. By 8 a.m., I'm stepping into the office lobby, appreciating the rare quiet of the early hour. The ding of the elevator signals its arrival, and as the doors slide open, I freeze.

Wren stands in the center of the car, her hair cascading in soft waves around her shoulders. The confined space suddenly feels too small. I step inside, keeping my distance, and press the button for the 12th floor. My eyes flick to the already illuminated 9th floor—her destination. Noted.

The silence between us is heavy, punctuated only by the hum of the elevator. I'm acutely aware of her presence, of every small shift she makes. When the doors open on her floor, she steps out without a backward glance, muttering just loud enough for me to hear: "Asshole."

The doors slide shut, and for a moment, I'm stunned. Then, to my own surprise, I smile.

Despite my best efforts, thoughts of Wren linger throughout the day. I replay our elevator encounter, her anger, the way her nose flares when she's upset. It's maddening. All I wanted this morning was to grab a fistful of her curls and kiss her senseless. But reality intrudes. I can't let my personal feelings cloud my judgment. I have to terminate her position. The board won't blame Eric, the golden boy partner, for the budget issues. They'll blame me—the one tasked with overseeing expenses. This isn't my mistake, but it's my responsibility to fix it.

A scheduled lunch with my sister Ayla offers a welcome reprieve. The bistro on the second floor is warm and inviting, the scent of fresh bread wafting through the air. Our corner table overlooks the city skyline, the soft afternoon light casting a golden glow. Ayla glides toward me, her denim-on-denim outfit as bold as her personality. She greets me with a kiss on the cheek, her cerulean eyes sparkling with excitement as she tears into a piece of bread from the basket.

"Guess what?" she announces, barely able to contain her grin.

"What?" I ask, amused by her enthusiasm.

"Dad joined Mom in therapy," she says, her smile widening. "And not just any therapy—couples' yoga therapy."

I nearly choke on my water. "Seriously?"

She laughs, nodding. "He said his back feels like he's 40 again. Whatever that means."

The image of my stoic father in a yoga pose is absurd, but the revelation is heartening. For years, their marriage has been strained, the little cracks in their relationship growing into gaping fissures. I'd noticed the signs—the absence of flowers Dad used to bring home, the special IPA Mom used to drive hours to get, the way they started inhabiting separate corners of the same house. Yet, somehow, they've found their way back to each other. It's a testament to the resilience of love, even when it feels like all is lost.

"What happens when an unstoppable force meets an immovable object?" I muse aloud, a small smile tugging at my lips.

Ayla grins, raising her glass. "Apparently, they go to couples' yoga."

We clink glasses, sharing a rare moment of levity. For now, at least, the weight of the world feels just a little lighter.

Seven

Hallway Intro's

Wren

February 11th

The pressure mounts with each passing day as I prep for the Valentine's Day social, my first event since being hired. The haunting knowledge of William's intent to fire me adds an extra layer of strain, but let me tell you, nothing—absolutely nothing—is going to stop me. This job isn't just a means to an end; it's my launchpad, my stepping stone toward Nest Designs, my future dream. I'm here to make a mark, save money for my own venture, and get my name out there. Each event I plan is like an audition for my dreams, a chance to shine and show the world exactly what I'm capable of. Dove built her bakery from scratch—through sweat, tears, and a whole lot of dough—and now she's about to open a second location. If she can do it, then so can I, with perseverance and a spirit that never backs down. The universe better make way for me, because I am coming through.

As lunchtime rolls around, my stomach decides it's time for a feast, and I make my way to the bistro on the second floor. No bustling elevators for me today; I'm taking the stairs, practically skipping two steps at a time. I need this lunch, and I need it now. The glass host stand greets me as I wait for acknowledgment, my eyes scanning the restaurant until they land on someone all too familiar: William. There he is, embracing the beautiful brunette woman I saw him with at the diner. My mood sours immediately. A surge of annoyance bubbles up in my chest, followed by an uncomfortable twist of jealousy. Who knew broody old William had this side of him? The soft smile he's giving her, the easy way he leans in his chair, those relaxed shoulders— I almost don't recognize him. He's not the thorn in my side I know from the office; he's a different person, calm, even charming. It leaves me both confused and annoyed.

Ugh. I hate him. Except I don't—not entirely. And that fact irritates me more than anything.

The host finally attends to me, and I quickly collect my lunch order and slip away before I have to deal with any awkward run-ins. I return to my desk, take a deep breath, and prepare myself for the chaos of my inbox. As I scroll through my missed calls and unread emails, one subject line makes my heart drop: "Valentine's Day Social Vendor Issue." I almost spit out my water. The drink vendor for the event is scheduled for the wrong date. How?! How could this happen when I meticulously double-checked everything? My pulse quickens as panic tries to seep in, but I squash it down. I do not have time to freak out.

Hesitantly, I move the cursor over to the next email, bracing myself. And, of course, it's another setback—the tablecloths I had specially ordered are delayed, no new delivery date in sight. Just the word "delayed" taunting me on the tracking page. Fantastic. Just fantastic. It feels like the universe is throwing curveballs my way, but guess what? I'm a batter, and I'm ready to hit it out of the park. I reach out to my sisters in the group chat, practically begging them to pull in any favors they can to get a drink vendor on board. The delayed tablecloths are a bummer, but drinks are essential, and that's where my focus is.

No time to waste. Driven by urgency, I make a beeline for the twenty-first floor—Eric's office. I'm not the type to back down, and I'm certainly not about to lose my job over something like this. As I walk in, his back is to me, his broad shoulders catching my attention for a brief moment. I know he hears the click of my heels because he turns around with a smile that starts off professional but quickly shifts to something genuine. I'm standing in his doorway, feeling a mix of determination and desperation, but I keep my chin up.

"Eric, I need your help," I say, straight to the point. I lay it all out for him—the drink vendor, the wrong date, the nightmare of it all. I'm trying to stay confident, but part of me can't help thinking I might be fired on the spot. I cross my arms and lean against the doorframe, waiting for him to come to his senses and give me the boot. The first event I plan, and here I am, already begging for help.

Eric stands, takes a few steps toward me, and gestures for me to come into his office. I step in, my pulse racing, stopping just a foot away from him. I brace myself.

"I'll take care of it. Someone owes me a favor," he says, leaning against his desk. He's so relaxed, so effortlessly comfortable, and here I am, practically a bundle of nervous energy. It takes me a second to process what he just said. He's helping me? My brows knit together, and I realize my jaw is dangerously close to dropping.

"Is there another problem?" Eric asks, dipping his head slightly, his eyes meeting mine.

I blink, clearing my thoughts. "Oh, no. That was all. I wasn't expecting such a quick fix, to be honest." I let out a deep exhale, tension slowly melting from my shoulders. I feel a spark of gratitude—a warmth spreading through me. Eric, with his thick midnight hair, those fitting brows, and that smile that's almost devilish—maybe he's not so bad after all.

"I'm here to help, Wren. If there's anything else you need, just let me know," he says, his smile widening, a daring sparkle in his eyes.

"Wow, thanks, Eric. Honestly, with William trying to kick me out of here on the next bus, I thought you'd be out of reach too."

"I'm always within your reach, Ms. Reese," he replies, and the double meaning is not lost on me. My cheeks warm slightly, and I glance away, trying to regain composure. But no matter how hard I try to find that spark for Eric, my thoughts are invaded by William—his infuriating stare, the way his jaw clenches when he's angry, the hands that gripped my shoulders with a fire that matched my own. Oh my God. I am standing in Eric's office, fantasizing about William. I clear my throat, and Eric is still watching me, his gaze polite yet suggestive.

"I really can't thank you enough, Eric!" The words come out more like a rush of emotion than an organized statement. Without thinking, I lunge forward, wrapping my arms around him in a hug. It isn't until I feel his broad chest against my cheek that I realize what I'm doing. He stiffens, surprised at first, then relaxes. I hear the pat of his hand on my lower back. Reality snaps me out of it—here I am, hugging Eric in his all-glass office during prime office hours.

"Oh my gosh, I am so sorry!" I start to pull away, but Eric grabs my arm, halting my retreat. His hand lifts my chin so I'm looking directly at him, his eyes now softer, warmer.

"Don't apologize. I was just caught off guard," he says, his voice low. There's a heat to his stare that sends a shiver up my spine. Everything in me begs me to spark that fire for Eric, to replace William's maddening cold void in my chest with Eric's warm support—but the heart doesn't work like that. If it did, we wouldn't need romance novels; it would all be too easy.

I manage a polite smile, my nerves lighting up like sparklers. Words fail me, so I awkwardly nod. Eric releases my arm, and I take one last lingering look before turning on my heel to exit. Just as I cross the threshold, Eric calls out one more time.

"You have a good day, Ms. Reese." The words themselves are professional, but his tone is anything but.

* * *

Arriving home, I need a reset. I make a beeline for my mom's art studio—a haven where I can let all this tension unravel. The room feels alive, bursting with colors, art supplies scattered across the floor, half-finished canvases leaning against the walls, and tiny trinkets that have stories of their own. My mother sits in her oversized tan recliner, knitting needles clicking rhythmically. She looks like she belongs in a fairy tale—Raven's old Penn hoodie and purple tie-dye leggings, sitting cross-legged like the queen of the creative kingdom.

"Hello, my songbird," she greets me, her voice soft and welcoming, with that melody that always brings me a sense of calm. She puts aside her knitting, looking at me with warmth and curiosity.

"Mom, I need to decorate the studio for Valentine's Day," I announce, settling at her feet, fiddling with my hands. My mom gives me a look—patient, understanding, but curious.

"You usually do, my love. Why mention it?" Her question is gentle, probing just enough to let me know she's aware something more is going on. She pulls me up and, with a small grunt, sets me in her lap. Even though she's smaller than me now, I still feel like a cub in her embrace, like nothing can hurt me here.

Her arms tighten around me, a bear hug that grounds me, and I exhale—a full-bodied, tension-releasing sigh. She lets me go, and I head to the wooden art supply table in the middle of the room. A few charcoal sticks lie scattered near an open water bill, and I pick one up, starting to sketch without much thought. My mom resumes her knitting, her needles clicking in time with my thoughts.

"I'm trying to build my portfolio," I say, drawing lines that I hope will lead to something meaningful. "I need variety, and, well… I'm just…" My voice trails off, weighed down by my own hesitations.

"Okay. Well, your father and I are here if you need help, my love," she reassures me, her warm smile like a beacon. Her fingers loop yellow yarn with effortless grace.

"Are you finally taking the big leap?" she asks nonchalantly, trying not to scare me off with too much enthusiasm. She knows me well. I cherish my parents; they're my rocks, my pillars of strength. They can be a little eccentric, sure, but they're amazing, and I'm grateful for them every day.

Their love story started with a shared passion for bird conservation— it's why we all have bird names, after all. What started as an adventure saving South America's declining bird population became a beautiful family. Now, they're more rooted, trading their traveling boots for family life. My dad writes historical fiction, and my mom's wellness studio is her haven, offering everything from postpartum healing to couples' yoga.

"I… am," I say, turning away, reaching for an eraser. My voice sounds hesitant, even to my own ears.

"I think that's terrific," she says, lifting herself from her recliner to hug me. She turns my head gently, her eyes meeting mine. "My songbird, there's nothing you could do that you wouldn't excel at. You are a bright, burning star in a world content with twinkles. Your doubts are just guardrails to keep you steady on your path."

"What made you open the studio? How did you know it would be successful?" I whisper, suddenly feeling small.

"Oh honey, I didn't!" she exclaims, laughing. She grabs a pencil, moving toward the easel.

"It was just one of many ideas I had that day," she says, sketching a bird. "I went to do yoga by the pond, but there was a kid's birthday party—clowns and all. I thought, wouldn't it be nice if there was a space, an oasis, just for yoga? So, I wrote the idea down, told your father, and we figured out the rest."

"Just like that?" I ask, shaking my head.

"Just like that," she says with a smile.

"I also considered being a chorus teacher. Didn't work out. And a bookstore-gaming café. Could you imagine? It was a great idea—half library, half gaming lounge, with a community space in the middle." She smiles, her eyes distant.

"Why didn't you do it?" I ask, sitting beside her easel.

"Interesting choice of words, my love. 'Follow through,'" she says, air quoting.

"Your path should call to you, like a siren's song. You can follow any path, but without following your true one, your soul will yearn for completion." She sweeps her hair into a bun, shading her sketch. "Your father, you girls, the studio—they all complete me. Any other path, and I'd only be half of who I am."

I sit with her words, letting them settle. She steps away from the easel, her masterpiece taking shape—a wren, wings outstretched, leaving a branch. I smile, resting my head atop hers.

"Do you know why we named you Wren?" she asks, breaking the silence.

I shake my head.

"You were strong, even in the womb. They worried you weren't turning in time, but I knew you—you just needed time. The night before the procedure, I walked and talked to you, sang to you. You kicked all night. By morning, you'd turned. You were no Robin; you were a Wren—fierce, determined, and ready."

I smile, tears stinging my eyes.

"I think I have a pretty great singing voice," I say, laughing.

"Oh my love, if only that were true," she teases, standing on her tiptoes to kiss my forehead.

Eight

The Day Before

Wren

February 13th

The morning unfolds with a chaotic symphony of mishaps—the unforgiving burn from the iron betraying my favorite blouse, the rebellion of the coffee maker that shorts out five minutes before I have to leave, and to top it off, a sudden downpour that plays havoc with my hair, transforming it into a frizzy halo of chaos. I brush a futile hand through my wild mane, resigning myself to the inevitable fate of a ballerina bun. With little time, I run up the stairs to the bathroom for a quick fix, slapping a glob of gel on my tresses and slicking it all back. I grab my strongest bow tie from around the bathroom door knob and begin twisting it around the hold I have on my locks. Curly hair is not easily put into a professionally appropriate bun; it's a battle, but I make it work just as my alarm blares, signaling it's time to leave.

Despite the rocky start, I manage to arrive at work ten minutes early, determined to conquer the day despite the hurdles. The office greets me in all its splendor, the vision from my sketchbook brought to life in vivid hues of pink and red that envelop the space in a warm embrace of love and festivity. Doubt lingers in the shadows of my mind, but as I take in the transformed spaces, a surge of pride swells within me. I really have outdone myself this time. The anticipation of tomorrow night's event propels me forward, a spark of excitement fueling my steps as I inspect each floor, my eagle eye searching for any overlooked detail that could mar the perfection of the evening.

Everything seems immaculate, each corner a testament to my careful planning and beautiful aesthetic. Seated at my desk, I glance out at the office space with a mix of disbelief and awe. The realization that I am living my dream, doing what I love in a space of creative freedom, washes over me. My mother was right—I do feel called to this. Maybe not in this exact setting—an office with limitations on the kind of events I can throw—but orchestrating grand visual experiences is my art. This is my calling. Taking an idea or a sentimental day and bringing it alive in every aspect, far beyond a party, and eliciting an entire experience.

Unfortunately, I have one floor I purposely overlooked—the twelfth floor. William's floor. While I managed to decorate it with the basics on the rare day William was out of the office for a client meeting, giving it matching decor to every other floor, it still feels bare. Rushing and paranoid that day, I didn't decorate the kitchen or lobby, leaving a lingering weight of worry until today. The urgency of the upcoming evaluation spurs me into action, steeling my resolve to face the Spawn of Satan before noon, unwilling to let any fear of a possible run-in create a flaw in my first big show of work.

Entering the kitchen on the twelfth floor, I make a beeline for the large mini fridge tucked in the corner, reaching in to grab a flavored seltzer water to combat my chaotic nerves simmering at the surface. Just as my hand hovers over the cool refreshment, the sound of footsteps echoes through the room, prompting me to straighten up and turn, only to be met with the sight of William standing at the entryway, his gaze fixed on me with that all-too-familiar blank expression that never fails to rile me up.

"What, are you staring at?" I quip, rolling my eyes in a mix of annoyance and intrigue.

"Thinking, not staring," William retorts, the effortless calm in his voice matching his nonchalant posture as he leans against the doorway.

His composure is infuriating, that self-assured aura surrounding him like an invisible shield. "Well, go think somewhere else, Will," I jest, grabbing a chair from the nearby table as if to emphasize my point.

"I would, if you weren't so distracting." He scoffs, helping himself to a banana from the hook beneath the white cabinet, his movements poised and smooth.

"That hasn't matured…" I tease, a mischievous glint in my eye as I throw a glance over my shoulder, a playful smirk curling at my lips.

"Excuse me?" William's sharp tone cuts through the air, a glint of confusion flashing in his eyes.

"The banana. It. Hasn't. Matured," I state with a smirk, watching as he glances down at the fruit in his hand, realization crossing his features before he replaces the banana with a nod to himself.

Despite my back turned to him now, I sense his lingering presence, the unspoken tension hanging heavy in the air as I resist the urge to turn and meet his gaze. I should've waited until after hours to decorate this floor. I shake my head, taking a sip of my seltzer, conflicting emotions swirling beneath the surface. But I don't need William, of all people, to know I'm one email away from a mental breakdown.

He continues to fade into shadow, the silence deafening. I swear I can hear his smirk crackling in the air. He's testing me, and for once, I have no slick remark, no quippy pun. I am a prisoner to his still resolve. Minutes pass, the silence stretching so long I begin to think he has finally left the kitchen. Unfortunately, my assumption is proven false as I turn, only to find him still there, his figure nonchalantly propped against the sleek white cabinets. Our eyes lock in an unspoken battle of wills, the tension crackling between us like static electricity. It's a delicate dance of push and pull.

"Why are you such an asshole?" I venture, the words tumbling out like a challenge, laced with a hint of curiosity.

"Am I?" he shoots back, a small grin playing on his lips as he crosses his arms deftly, his gaze unwavering in its intensity.

"You don't speak, and when you do, it's rude nothings," I retort, frustration pounding in my temples.

"Would you like me to speak more?" he offers, a brow raised in amusement, stepping subtly forward from the cabinets, subtracting some very necessary distance between us.

"I think you're missing the point," I counter, shifting in my seat to better meet his gaze, a spark of defiance flickering in my eyes as they remain locked on his. I will not back down. He may try this brute act with everyone else, but I am not everyone else.

"And what is your point, Wren?" he queries, swaying his hand in front of him.

"My point is, you want me fired without even knowing me. You walk around all silent and brooding, and the moment I think I'm free of you, there you are!" I declare, a flood of indignation echoing in my raised voice, now standing, taking strides toward him.

As he closes the distance between us, a surge of conflicting emotions swirls within me—a potent mix of anger, desire, and defiance colliding in a tempestuous storm. The urge to lash out wavers as a stronger, more forbidden desire burns fiercely within me—the overwhelming yearning for his touch, his kiss. I turn my head to the side, rejecting the consuming thoughts of his lips on me.

William leans in, his breath ghosting along the line of my neck, his voice a deep, soft whisper that caresses my ear, "I too, am your captive, Wren." The words send a jolt through me, a potent cocktail of tension and lust electrifying the space between us. Our eyes meet in a silent exchange, his amber gaze flecked with hints of gold revealing a vulnerability beneath the layers of armor he wears. Before I can fully process the moment, a roar of clapping from outside the kitchen interrupts us, jolting us both back to reality. With a swift step to the side, he withdraws, then continues to exit the kitchen.

* * *

Arriving home, I need a reset. Again. I make a beeline for my mom's art studio—a haven where I can let all this tension unravel. The room feels alive, bursting with colors, art supplies scattered across the floor, half-finished canvases leaning against the walls, and tiny trinkets that have stories of their own. My mother sits in her over-sized tan recliner, crochet needle clicking against her nails rhythmically. She looks like she belongs in a fairy tale—Raven's old Penn bright pink hoodie and purple tie-dye leggings, sitting cross-legged like the queen of the creative kingdom.

"Hello, my songbird," she greets me, her voice soft and welcoming, with that melody that always brings me a sense of calm. She puts aside her project, looking at me with warmth and curiosity.

"Mom, I need to decorate the studio for Valentine's Day," I announce, settling at her feet, fiddling with my hands. My mom gives me a look—patient, understanding, but curious.

"You usually do, my love. Why mention it?" Her question is gentle, probing just enough to let me know she's aware something more is going on. She pulls me up and, with a small grunt, sets me in her lap. Even though she's smaller than me now, I still feel like a cub in her embrace, like nothing can hurt me here.

Her arms tighten around me, a bear hug that grounds me, and I exhale—a full-bodied, tension-releasing sigh. She lets me go, and I head to the wooden art supply table in the middle of the room. A few charcoal sticks lie scattered near an open water bill, and I pick one up, starting to sketch without much thought. My mom resumes her crocheting, her needle clicking in time with my thoughts.

"I'm trying to build my portfolio," I say, drawing lines that I hope will lead to something meaningful. "I need variety, and, well… I'm just…" My voice trails off, weighed down by my own hesitations.

"Okay. Well, your father and I are here if you need help, my love," she reassures me, her warm smile like a beacon. Her needle looping through yellow yarn with effortless grace.

"Are you finally taking the big leap?" she asks nonchalantly, trying not to scare me off with too much enthusiasm. She knows me well. I cherish my parents; they're my rocks, my pillars of strength. They can be a little eccentric, sure, but they're amazing, and I'm grateful for them every day.

Their love story started with a shared passion for bird conservation—it's why we all have bird names, after all. What started as an adventure saving South America's declining bird population became a beautiful family. Now, they're more rooted, trading their traveling boots for family life. My dad writes historical fiction, and my mom's wellness studio is her haven, offering everything from postpartum healing to couples' yoga.

"I… am," I say, turning away, reaching for an eraser. My voice sounds hesitant, even to my own ears.

"I think that's terrific," she says, lifting herself from her recliner to hug me. She turns my head gently, her eyes meeting mine. "My songbird, there's nothing you could do that you wouldn't excel at. You are a bright, burning star in a world content with twinkles. Your doubts are just guardrails to keep you steady on your path."

"What made you open the studio? How did you know it would be successful?" I whisper, suddenly feeling small.

"Oh honey, I didn't!" she exclaims, laughing. She grabs a pencil, moving toward the easel.

"It was just one of *many* ideas I had that day," she says, sketching a bird. "I went to do yoga by the pond, but there was a kid's birthday party—clowns and all. I thought, wouldn't it be nice if there was a space, an oasis, just for yoga? So, I wrote the idea down, told your father, and we figured out the rest."

"Just like that?" I ask, shaking my head.

"Just like that," she says with a smile.

"I also considered being a chorus teacher. Didn't work out. And a bookstore-gaming café. Could you imagine? It was a great idea—half library, half gaming lounge, with a community space in the middle." She smiles, her eyes distant.

"Why didn't you follow through?" I ask, sitting beside her easel.

"Interesting choice of words, my love. 'Follow through,'" she says, air quoting.

"Your path should call to you, like a siren's song. You can follow any path, but without following your true one, your soul will yearn for completion." She sweeps her hair into a bun, shading her sketch. "Your father, you girls, the studio—they all complete me. Any other path, and I'd only be half of who I am."

I sit with her words, letting them settle. She steps away from the easel, her masterpiece taking shape—a wren, wings outstretched, leaving a branch. I smile, resting my head atop hers.

"Do you know why we named you Wren?" she asks, breaking the silence.

I shake my head.

"You were strong, even in the womb. They worried you weren't turning in time, but I knew you—you just needed time." she paused and smiled, "The night before the procedure to turn you themselves, I walked and talked to you, sang to you. You kicked all night. By morning, you'd turned. You were no Robin like we'd plan to name you; you were a Wren—my little song bird."

I smile, tears stinging my eyes.

"If only, you could hold a note." my mom joked.

"I think I have a pretty great singing voice," I say, laughing.

"Oh my love, if only that were true," she teases, standing on her tiptoes to kiss my forehead.

Nine

Valentine's Day

Wren

February 14th

As I chaotically arrange the emergency booklet I crafted for every event, the soft hum of anticipation fills my office. I've accounted for every disaster, even an earthquake. Tonight will go exactly as planned. I brought a change of clothes so I don't have to leave to get ready for the party, selecting the perfect two options, once again planning for any disaster. My first option is a dark pink maxi dress with a sweetheart neckline, and while it's not backless, it accentuates my shoulders, back, and neck. The second option is a red-on-red floral midriff bustier dress that flows down to my shins. I packed two pairs of shoes as well, one for each dress.

I look to the walls covered with hearts, streamers cascading down the door frame—I've poured my heart and soul into every aspect of the Valentine's Day party. Darren and Caroline have found me twice today to compliment the office decor and the theme: "Baby Cupid Stole My Heart." I didn't want to make the theme couple-oriented, knowing it could be a trigger for someone single this year. Glancing at the clock, I realize the event is only two hours away. Whoo-sah.

A soft knock on my office door pulls my attention from the clock. Eric, wearing a fitted dark burgundy suit and an unbuttoned blush pink shirt, stands framed in the doorway. Wow. His crisp suits always exude authority, but the way he stares into my eyes without breaking eye contact is the power struggle I adore. His stare is bedazzling. I break the connection and look back down at my checklist.

"Quite the transformation in here," he remarks, his gaze lingering on the heart-shaped garlands hanging from the ceiling above the aisles of cubicles. I smile, nerves fluttering beneath my composed exterior. "Thank you. I wanted to create an atmosphere that really captures the essence of Valentine's Day... without going overboard, of course."

He steps closer, his eyes tracing the office floor. "You've certainly succeeded. It's tasteful, elegant, and," he pauses, his gaze meeting mine with a subtle intensity, "quite enchanting." My heartbeat quickens at the unexpected compliment, and I stammer out a response. "I appreciate that, Mr. Pearson. I want to make sure everyone has a memorable evening."

Eric is not the uptight boss type, so I don't know why I'm so on edge and robotic. His lips curl into a faint smile, a glint of something more lingering in his eyes. "I'm sure it will be memorable for everyone."

I feel a subtle heat rise to my cheeks at his response. A surprising attraction peaks, and I bat my lashes, releasing a genuine smile. As my nose crinkles and I bite my bottom lip to keep from grinning foolishly, Eric's eyes dilate. His face loses its boyish charm, revealing a hunger. I clear my throat to break the tension, and his golden retriever smile slides back on. He lingers for a moment longer before excusing himself with a firm, "I'll see you tonight, Ms. Reese."

The seventh floor of our office building has undergone a mesmerizing transformation, courtesy of Nest Designs. I just love saying that—well, thinking it, as I have yet to tell anyone officially. As I step into the space, I'm immediately captivated by the whimsy of our cupid-inspired extravaganza. Strands of twinkling fairy lights hang by the entrance, casting a warm glow on the cupid-themed decor within. The walls are adorned with golden bows and arrows, creating a delicate dance of shadows against a backdrop of crimson and blush hues. Heart-shaped balloons float along the floor, creating a symphony of love, while a gentle mist of rose-scented air lingers in the atmosphere.

The centerpiece I chose for the celebration is nothing short of magical: a life-sized ice sculpture of Cupid, poised with his bow drawn and an impish grin. Yup, an ice sculpture. Surrounded by an alluring garden of faux roses and lush greenery, Cupid commands attention and sets the tone for the evening. Each table is topped with meticulously arranged bouquets of red, pink, and white flowers. The tablecloths are a baby pink, almost looking white under the lights. Seeing it all together, I'm in love. It's perfect.

Mission: complete.

Standing near the appetizer table, Darren is beside me, wearing a pink sweater with tan khakis and pink Ugg boots. He's talking about his most recent Hinge match as the elevator doors slide open, revealing the gallant figure of William stepping onto the seventh floor. My breath momentarily catches in my throat. The dim glow of the soft overhead lights frames him, casting a dark magnetic allure that elevates him beyond the ordinary. Right now, my dislike for him subsides as I fully take him in, every detail meticulously in place—from the perfectly tailored garnet suit that accentuates his broad shoulders, draped over a black button-up, to the subtle gleam in his eyes. He licks his lips just before turning his head to scan the crowd, and I burn with the desire to take that bottom lip into my mouth and bite. Suck. Lick… until his hard shell shatters. I shake off my lust and refocus on Darren's speech about dating apps needing a review feature.

* * *

William

I've never seen this office look so wonderful for Valentine's Day, or any day to be frank. You'd never guess that most of the people here are usually buried beneath the weight of their daily miseries. I suppose her role as the office decorator does mean something. Standing in the center of chatter with Cody and Martin, we discuss the Super Bowl, but it's a mere hum in the background. My attention is fixated on her. She glides through the party like an angel, effortlessly capturing attention and elevating the evening. The way she moves, the grace in her step, it's captivating. I pretend to survey the crowd, but my eyes are drawn back to her every few seconds. She catches my gaze once and rolls her eyes, as if to punctuate the absurdity of my attempt at subtlety.

As the night wears on, the party begins to wind down. Most have left, and only the divorced partners and the inebriated assistants remain—a reason I would have left hours ago. Yet, with Wren still in attendance, I can't bring myself to leave. She's at the bar, engrossed in fixing the tiny heart-covered umbrellas, even though no one left is sober enough to criticize anything at this point.

Eric saunters up to Wren, and they laugh and converse for a few minutes, all while he looks at her like she hung the moon. While she laughs at whatever he said, I recognize she has a wall up. Wren, as much as she outwardly opposes me, is just like me in a way: scared to let someone get close, scared of someone seeing beneath the surface. Despite her suggestive body language, it's just an act she's perfected. His hand rests on the middle to lower part of Wren's back to guide her, but she turns out of his grip effortlessly. She responds with a disarming smile, gracefully brushing off his advances and bidding him goodbye, making her way to Caroline. That's my girl.

As she begins to dance with Caroline, my eyes fixate on her sensual movements. The glow on her golden brown skin, her long smooth legs, that dress—accentuating every curve. She's stunning.

Wren's hair bounces over her shoulders as she shakes her head to the music while stepping off the dance floor. God, I dream of the day I get to fist that hair. In that moment, everyone else in the room fades. The lights fall upon Wren, and as if she can feel me, she looks up mindlessly, instantly locking eyes with me. Shock is her first reaction at the crackling energy between us, then her gaze becomes impassive, mirroring my own. I want to hold the stare, continue this dance, but I'm not sure I can control my eyes from revealing everything my mouth won't. So, hating myself for it, I look away indifferently.

The DJ's announcement that it's the last song signals the end of the night. Reluctantly, I leave and head to the garage, where Randy from accounting, Darren from management, and a few stragglers join me in the elevator. We all exit on the third floor, making our way to our respective cars. Now out of the elevator, it's then that I feel a tingling crawl up my back. I can feel her staring at me, even though I didn't see her enter the elevator before me—my body knows with certainty she is behind me.

I turn abruptly, thinking to say something, anything, but words escape me. I look down at her, our eyes locked, hers wide with surprise. The tension in the air thickens. My jaw clenches, and I feel the weight of my anger, my frustration. I don't know what to say; she hates me, that much I am certain of. She's probably right to. I know I come across as rough, uncaring—a brute. And maybe I am. Maybe that's all I'll ever be. I don't know why I turned around, no plan—just an impulsive reaction based on dumb lust and something darker, a need to claim her attention, her defiance. Unable to find the right words, I sigh heavily, the sound almost a growl, and turn away, walking to my car and getting in without uttering a single syllable.

* * *

Wren

The weight of the night finally lifts as the party comes to an end. While planning the event was enjoyable, the accompanying stress felt like a relentless burden. This is good though, I'm learning the ups and downs of the business. Chasing your dream isn't all happy times and Pinterest quotes; there's going to be some adversity. Fortunately, the night was perfect, not one problem arose. Everyone complimented me on the theme and the decor—there were so many inquiries for my services I almost got tired of saying Nest Designs. Almost. But I am so proud of myself. I doubted if my hobby could be a profession, and tonight was all the validation I needed.

Standing in the elevator, I watch William step on, his gaze fixed straight ahead. Engaging in light banter with Darren, I try to shake off the remnants of the night. As we exit the elevator, William walks ahead, seemingly oblivious to my presence. Darren, caught up in sharing details about his new date, says,

"I don't know, the convo was alright, but the kiss, the kiss was everything."

"How's the ass?" I joke, playfully nudging his shoulder with mine. At that very moment, William turns around, locking eyes with me. I stop mid-laugh, flustered by the unexpected intensity of his gaze. I can feel my cheeks heat up, and my smile falters for a split second. He doesn't say a word. Darren looks between us, mirroring the confusion that clouds my own thoughts. William shifts his gaze from me to Darren and back to me before abruptly turning around and leaving, getting into his car.

Did he hear my joke? Was that inappropriate to say at work? Oh crap, did I offend him? Technically it's after work hours, so he can't add this to my rap sheet. I shake my head and laugh at myself—what's he gonna do, file an HR complaint about a butt joke? I climb into the car with Darren, patiently waiting for his engine to hum to life so I can connect my phone to Bluetooth. After a night filled with radio tunes and oldies at the party, I'm eager to indulge in my own playlist.

"Hey, Darren, mind if we turn up the volume? I need something to wipe that awkwardness off my brain," I say, trying to lighten the mood.

"Sure thing, Wren. You do have a killer taste in music," Darren replies with a grin, and I roll my eyes playfully.

Darren drops me off in front of my house. I thank him for the ride and get out of the silver Honda. My house, unusually well-lit for 10 PM, catches my attention. Caution creeps into my steps as I survey the block before cautiously ascending the steps of my parents' home. I stopped being comfortable calling it "my home" when I moved back after my breakup. This is their space, and I feel the unspoken pressure to find my own. My parents, understanding and supportive, would never kick me out, but I understand they need their space back.

"Okay, Wren, stop being dramatic," I whisper to myself as I reach the door. "It's just lights. Maybe they forgot to turn them off."

Opening the door, I'm greeted by an explosion of poppers and streamers. With the key still in the door, I stand there in shock, wondering what's going on. Snapping out of my daze, I see my parents, sisters, aunt, and uncle standing in the living room. A banner above the kitchen entry reads, "Happy Birthday" with "birthday" crossed out and replaced with "First Event." It finally dawns on me—they've orchestrated a surprise celebration for my successful party planning. Overwhelmed with emotion, I remove my keys and step inside.

First to embrace me are my parents, followed by my aunt and uncle. My sisters join in, jumping on me with laughter and screams. I can't help but laugh along, my heart swelling with gratitude. Even Raven, usually the most reserved of us all, wears a contented smile and gifts me a chic business card holder.

"Raven, is this real leather?" I tease, raising an eyebrow.

She rolls her eyes. "Of course, it is. Only the best for the rising star of Nest Designs," she says with a smirk, and I can't help but pull her into another hug.

Shedding my coat and shoes, I make my way through the crowd to the kitchen island, where an array of my favorite foods await—a bowl of Kit Kats, a white cheese pizza with jalapeños, popcorn mixed with M&Ms, and homemade lemon drops.

"Oh my God, you guys really went all out!" I exclaim, my eyes widening at the spread.

"Well, we know how to celebrate a Wren-sized victory," my dad says, winking at me.

My mom and aunt are engaged in conversation in the living room, while my sisters bombard me with questions about the office party.

"Did everyone love the decor?" Raven asks, her eyes wide with excitement.

"Yeah, yeah, and tell us if anyone hit on you!" Lark adds with a sly grin.

"Of course, they loved it. I mean, did you see what I did with those heart-shaped garlands? But no, no hitting on, just compliments," I reply, giving them a playful glare. "And maybe a little flirting, but nothing serious."

"Typical Wren, always charming but never settling," Dove teases, and I stick my tongue out at her.

The atmosphere is filled with so much joy and support, and I mentally and verbally thank my family for the perfect ending to my big day. This is exactly what I needed—a reminder that no matter how chaotic things get, I've got a whole team cheering me on. And if nothing else, I know that with them by my side, I can handle anything.

Ten

Cold Springs

William

March 11th

The first day of spring arrives with an unexpected twist—snow blankets the city, shutting down schools and offices. I find solace in the silence of the snowfall. It feels like the world pauses, and my mind follows suit. It's freezing, but I'm sweating profusely under my black snow coat and heavy-duty gloves. I'm shoveling snow not just in front of my place but also for my elderly neighbor, Carmen. I'm drowning in thoughts. While hundreds of micro-scenarios pass through my head during the hard work, one in particular repeats: *Wren.*

Jerry Smith, my four-legged bestfriend and I stay outside far longer than intended after shoveling; he loves the snow. I gather him out of the 2-foot hole he's currently reveling in, wiping his coat clean. He's a ball of gray and white fur with a red sweater my mom gifted him last Christmas. We embark on a post-shoveling walk, Jerry Smith shaking the remaining snow from his coat once I put him down on the newly cleared sidewalk.

An hour later, I call my dad, only to learn that he and Mom are vacationing in Florida. Those two are conundrums.

Dialing Ayla, I sense a shift in her tone immediately as she picks up.

"Hey," I say hesitantly. She hasn't said a word, yet I can already tell something is wrong.

A few dry beats pass, and Jerry Smith begins to twirl around in the snow as I stand at the stop sign up the street from my house. His nose is wet, and he's looking up at me with his head tipped to the side. He's probably sensing my anxiety over Ayla.

"I spoke with Mom and Dad…" I say, hoping she becomes chatty as usual about our parents' rollercoaster marriage at this moment.

"Yeah, they're in Orlando. Mom wanted to visit Disney—she's never been," she says, her voice cold and distant.

"Disney? An overpriced walkathon," I huff.

"Yeah, the lines are hours long. I don't see the appeal either," she retorts. This is wrong. Ayla is a Disney adult; she likes the frilly things in life. What is wrong with her?

"Are you okay?" I say, hating that I have to ask because she's just going to say, "I'm fine," in one, two, three…

"I'm fine, William," she sighs.

"Ay…" I reply. Could it be school? Is it one of her dumb friends? I know she doesn't really date, so I doubt it's her love life. I wince just thinking about Ayla dating; I don't care how old she gets, her dating is always news to me.

"I'm sorry, I've got to go… love you," she says, and before I can answer, the call ends.

Returning home, I walk up the shoveled path with fresh snow dusting over it. I stop on the porch, remove Jerry Smith's leash, and dust off his mittens protecting his paws. The snow has begun to fall again, but I salted the path, so I shouldn't have to shovel again—hopefully. I reach into my pocket and pull out my house keys. As I go to slide the key into the lock, my door slowly opens. I know I locked this door.

Shifting on both feet, I look up from the snow footprints on my welcome mat and scan my home. My eyes stop and focus on the figure in the unlit corner of my living room. Orange hair and a cinnamon beard. Hard eyes staring right at me. Marcus, my best friend since fifth grade, sits in my living room, on my couch, arms crossed—an unusual sight considering he lives an hour away, is typically engrossed in surgeries all day, and, most importantly, my door was supposed to be locked.

Entering the living room and eyeing the area, I stop. Removing my shoes, I lift a brow and glare at Marcus. "What are you doing here?" I demand.

Marcus grins, playful, forever donning the mask of a jokester. "Well, I may have taken a little break from my busy schedule to surprise you," he responds, showcasing a devilish grin.

Marcus stands and begins to approach me. "In a snowstorm? I thought you had an important surgery this week," I reply, turning my back to him to hang my coat and Jerry Smith's sweater. Marcus shrugs. "Something like that, but it was postponed due to some error with the patient's labs. I needed a break from all the scrubs and sterile environments anyway."

I know this is abnormal behavior for Marcus. He loves his job; he wouldn't be playing hooky for no reason. I turn to face him, smirking. "So, what brings the renowned Dr. O'Malley to my humble abode?"

Marcus's eyes dart to the right, then to the left. "Just wanted to see if you wanted to grab a beer," he says, pointing to the kitchen behind him. I'm looking at him, and while his mask is tightly secured, I know Marcus is only here because something is wrong. So, I'll play the game. I'll grab the beer, then he'll tell me what's going on.

Suddenly, Marcus catches me in a headlock, his arm wrapping tightly around my neck. Out of instinct, I grab at his arm with my right hand and struggle briefly before managing to twist my body to face him, smiling. I see Marcus shifting on his feet, readying himself. He's smiling back at me. While the headlock wasn't too tight, it still alerted my sensory system, which has my body crackling with adrenaline.

Now this—this is something I can get behind. I need to let off some steam with all the chaos at work. Knowing Marcus, this is exactly what he needs as well. Words are hard for us; that we have in common. When faced with pressure, an intense workout is the fix, and if that doesn't work, find someone to fight… or something else.

Marcus steps back and begins to pedal to the left while I methodically step right. "Prepare yourself, my copper friend. This might be more intense than your little operating room," I say, jumping at him just a bit to see if he reacts.

Marcus laughs. "I highly doubt that, Billy boy."

He swings again, and I duck left, grabbing his waist with both arms in a bear-hug-like move. My face is deep in Marcus's core, and I squeeze him tighter, but not enough to break his ribs. Marcus responds by slamming his closed fist down on my back like a gorilla. I spin around his waist, now hugging his back, strengthening my grip even more, and squat even lower. In a flash, I've successfully flipped him over my head and onto the floor, softening the blow by keeping hold of his core and slowing down at impact. Marcus squirms and kicks out his right foot, sweeping my feet from under me. My back hits the floor first, and the wind comes out of me in one big gust. We both lay there, breathing heavily. I chuckle and then begin to sit up, grabbing for his legs, and he laughs. Kicking his legs out, he taps the floor hard repeatedly, shouting, "Okay, okay, you win. I'm outmatched in the world of living room combat."

I let him go, and he sits up, mirroring my breathing. "Surgeon or not, your hands still aren't quick enough, boy," I say as we grab each other's arms to help stand up together.

"Remind me not to hold back next time," Marcus says while swiping at his pants, attempting to clear the wrinkles. Patting Marcus on the back, I say, "Next time, don't take a break from saving lives to challenge me. Now, talk. What's the real reason for this surprise visit?"

"Well, maybe I just missed my favorite slice of pie from that deli two blocks away, or maybe I needed the drive," Marcus says, grabbing the hair on the back of his neck.

"In the snow?" I say sarcastically.

"Will," he begins, a thoughtful expression on his face, "there's something I've got to tell you."

I raise my eyebrow, curiosity piqued. "Spill it, Marcus. You're not usually one for dramatic pauses." A smile plays on his lips as he reveals, "I'm moving back to Merritt City."

The words hang in the air, and I feel a rush of surprise and excitement. Marcus, the renowned surgeon with a thriving career at one of the biggest surgical centers on this side of the country, is coming back to the city where we grew up. "What? Why?" I blurt out, unable to hide my enthusiasm. Marcus chuckles. "Well, I've secured a chief surgical position at WMCMC, the West Merritt City Medical Center. It's a fantastic opportunity, and I couldn't pass it up."

"Where do you plan on living?" I ask, concern barely breaking into my impassive tone.

Marcus mindlessly nods. "I've been caught up in the details of the decision, and finding a place slipped my mind. I'm working on it, though."

"Somewhere to live wasn't on the list of details?" I quickly retort.

"I found a nice little box off of Rosedale and Main, front little patch of grass and everything," Marcus jokes.

"You can crash in one of my guest bedrooms until you find a place," I say, ignoring his joke.

He grins, then drops to a serious tone. "You sure about that?"

I chuckle. "Yeah, don't sweat it."

After a moment of contemplation, Marcus agrees. "Alright, but just for a while. I'll find my own place soon."

We settle on a six-month stay—enough time for Marcus to test the waters at the new hospital and decide if the move is the right choice. The idea of him staying under my roof brings a sense of companionship I hadn't realized I was missing. Loner by nature, I enjoy solitude. It takes a certain type of person to make me feel comfortable, and Marcus has always been that person. While he had plenty of friends growing up, he always stuck by my side. Me, the quiet tall boy with glasses. While we both played sports and got good grades, I wasn't social like Marcus. I wasn't social at all, really. There was always more going on in my head as a kid, guess I still hadn't figured out how to sort it yet.

* * *

Wren

I shiver under my blanketed fortress and peek my head out, looking for any liquid nearby. Unfortunately, I left my handy-dandy water bottle downstairs with my sisters. Damn, I have to get up. It's one of those days when the entire city will shut down, victim to Mother Nature's whims, and I fully intended to catch up on some good shut-eye. I love the snow in theory; I love the aura of warmth it brings, even though that contradicts its very presence. Snow makes everything beautiful—so mesmerizing, yet lethally dangerous—such a breathtaking dichotomy. It's a little late in the year for snow on the East Coast, but we only got one snowstorm this winter, so I'll take my losses with my wins. I check my phone for any new notifications. As I predicted, the entire city is basically at a standstill, even with all the preventative measures taken last night.

Raven and Dove slept over after the news stations began alerting businesses and citizens to shut down and prepare. Time spun back to when we were all in our teens, laughing and gossiping. Lark was braiding our hair while Raven spilled the tea on her coworkers we've never met. Dove, who was suspiciously missing for an hour or two, returned with our Creativity Box, and nostalgia whipped me back to my twelve-year-old self, with a big untamed mane and purple braces.

The Creativity Box was my parents' idea of an outlet for whenever we got angry. If any of us fought, bickered, or maybe cut up Raven's favorite sweater—ya know, sister stuff—we'd have to go to the large orange box and create. The box contained any miscellaneous art object you could think of: fabric, paint, tools, mini canvases, glass, flowers, and more. After you finished your creation, you'd have to gift your thoughtful and time-consuming masterpiece to the person who had been harmed by your action. No matter how embarrassing that gift-giving interaction was, the receiver of the gift would have to thank you and say one thing they liked about the gift.

It was **torture**.

We all circled the table as Dove placed the large box down. She unlocked the hatch and flipped the top open; with an eerie creak, the contents of the box came into view. To my surprise, everything was still there, completely unaffected by ten years of abandonment. Drawing materials were strewn across the coffee table, and the melody of our collective chatter echoed through the space. Memories of past winters flooded back, and it felt as if time had folded upon itself, allowing us to be carefree girls once more.

You never realize how much 'adulting' sucks until you reach the point the thirteen-year-old you prayed to be.

The more I watched Dove, the more I noticed a glow about her. With a subtle twinkle in her eye, she smiled as Raven finished her breakup story—obviously not hearing a word Raven said. Ray and David were over again, but it was truly no love lost for Raven. She allowed this on-again, off-again relationship with David to continue because it's really all she had time for. My sister doesn't want kids, doesn't want the big house; she wants to be on Forbes 40 under 40. She complains that her ambition to break personal career barriers makes dating impossible. I don't know about that. Raven is busy… but she makes time for us, which means she could make time for a partner.

In my opinion, she's a workaholic, constantly craving elevation in her career. She gets a high from achieving promotions. I'm very proud of her drive and discipline; I just wish she'd open herself up to the idea that love can be fulfilling too. I might not have experienced real love firsthand, but I'm still a hopeless romantic, and I still think everyone has that someone out there.

"Okay, spill it, Dovey. What's the deal?" Lark prompted, asking the question on all of our minds. Dove hesitated for a moment, a smile playing on her lips.

"Whatever do you mean?" Dove replied coyly.

"Mhm," Raven immediately interjects.

"There's a… how do you say… I got some—" Lark says while rubbing her chin and panning across all of us for a word she cannot grasp.

"Ah!" I say, snapping, and winking at Lark.

"Dick." They all snap their attention to me, Lark sharing a knowing smile.

"There's an 'I got some dick' energy radiating off of you!" I state loudly, then break my seriousness with a chuckle. Raven playfully slaps Dove's arm and says, "I smelled it the second you walked in here… it's all in that devilish little smile, like you're still thinking about it." Dove's grin spreads as she looks afar, and we all unite as sisters to gag.

"Please do not go all Splash Mountain while we're standing right here," Lark laughs. Dove's devilish grin returns to its natural form of a shy smile, like she's locking up the little fantasy she was just playing out in her mind.

"Well, I've got a… guy in my life."

Gasps of excitement filled the room as we bombarded her with questions, eager to learn more about the comet that had barreled through her insanely high walls. Dove, usually reserved about her personal life, began to open up, venting how this relationship marked a turning point for her. We all sat, jaws hanging, as she spoke with school-girl love in her eyes. We were all speechless, afraid our response would scare her back into the closet of secrecy she usually hid in.

"After the divorce, I wasn't sure if I'd ever take that chance, ya know… on love again," she confessed, letting her blondish-white curls fall in her face. "But he's different, and I finally feel ready. He makes me feel ready… He makes me feel seen… ya know? In a way I didn't know I could be seen. I thought there were always supposed to be pieces of you hidden, giving only the best parts on offer, but he's seen my ugly. And I, his."

Raven, Lark, and I were pale with shock, each feature softening as Dove's poetic words settled in. Dove was in love. *Real love.* Marrying your high school sweetheart might seem like a fairy tale, but the reality is often more nuanced. People evolve, and sometimes, so do their paths—which had been the case for Dove, unfortunately, with her ex-husband. After their divorce, she seemed to have cut herself off from any romantic connection.

"That is amazing, Dovey," I squeal, hugging her tightly. She laughs under my squeeze. Lark and Raven join in on the hug and squeeze harder. Then Dove bites my arm, I squirm to get from under Lark's hold, and we all release each other, laughing.

As the laughter settled, we found ourselves sitting quietly for a moment, each of us lost in our thoughts. Dove's confession had shifted something in the room—a sense of hope, of possibility. It reminded us that even in the face of life's challenges, love could still surprise us. The snowfall outside had grown heavier, and I looked toward the window, watching the flakes dance in the wind. The world felt hushed, like it was holding its breath for whatever came next.

"Well," Lark said, breaking the silence, "I think it's time we made some hot cocoa and figured out our next masterpiece with the Creativity Box. Who's with me?"

We all cheered in agreement, the atmosphere lighter now, and stood up to head to the kitchen. As we gathered the mugs and cocoa mix, I couldn't help but feel that today wasn't just a snow day—it was a day that reminded us of who we were and who we could still become.

Eleven

Multiple Choice

Wren

March 18th

Buzzing with the success of the St. Patrick's Day party, I was already planning the next celebration: National Pet Day on April 11th. Picture this: the office packed with furry companions, an opportunity for everyone to showcase their softer side. Eric, who informed me he owns a Calico named Misses, gave me the green light for my pet-friendly vision, including the ingenious portable potties from "Liana's Muddy Buddies."

Lunchtime beckoned, and I decided to take a break at the nearby café. Lost in my musings, I collided with an unexpected obstacle in the hallway—William's chest. Great. Holding me still by my shoulders with his large, strong hands, he looked down and whispered in his deep, powerful voice, "Eyes up, Wren."

Before the smallest hint of attraction could take root, William squashed it with his blank, indifferent stare. *I think I hate him.* His chocolate eyes were ice-cold, but just before I looked away, something flickered deep within them. I saw a burning afar—a glimmer of gold near his iris that held me captive, stuck wandering his brown pools for more perfect imperfections. I broke the trance and looked away, wondering why he hadn't walked off.

His usual confusing act didn't dampen my spirits this time. We stood there, his hands still on my shoulders, time seemingly stopping for us. I looked over my shoulder and back at him. He was still staring right at me with this searching yet intense glare that puzzled me.

"Can you let me go?" I said, and instantly he released me, taking one small step back. He didn't leave, though, and even while my mind was telling me to run, my body hadn't moved an inch. Drowning in the awkward silence, my mouth blurted out the first thing it could form.

"April 11th is Pet Day," I spilled out quicker than I could stop myself.

"Is it?" he inquired, still standing only inches away. Yet the way his head tipped ever so slightly to the side told me I'd piqued his interest.

"Yes, there will be an office party where employees can bring in their pets. It should be really fun! An email was sent out this week, I believe." Sharing the details of Pet Day seemed to soften his edges, and what came next surprised me even more.

"I'll bring in Jerry Smith," he said flatly, still eyeing me with an intensity I didn't understand.

"Wait…you named your pet after Rick & Morty? I love that show!" I said, letting loose a grin.

The flicker in his eyes was back, brighter, but once again only briefly. He rubbed his jaw and cast a look over my shoulder. I would love to be in that head of his. I could see a thousand gears turning, but his face gave no tell. It was sort of frustrating. I'm used to reading people so easily, but he's so different.

"Yes. My dog. Rick & Morty is my favorite animated series as well," he affirmed.

I began to laugh. I would never have expected him to have a dog, let alone with such a funny name. Usually, dog people are friendly to some level, and William is anything but. As I laughed, he eyed me like I was the puzzle I thought he was. I laughed so hard that I bent over, clutching my stomach, and I couldn't resist touching his arm for stability. Picturing him watching Rick & Morty on the couch, scowling, one hand petting this imaginary dog almost put me in tears.

As I began to uncurl with my smile at its widest, I felt his eyes before I saw them. And poof! All the air was sucked out of the place. The shift in his demeanor was shocking—frozen and angered? Like a switch, the conversation turned serious. Was this even a conversation? I never know with him. His eyes held no answers, as usual, and in embarrassment, I quickly retreated, turning on my heels and leaving him standing in the hallway.

Back at my desk, I delved into work, ensuring everything was in order for the arrival of the company emblem water bowls next Tuesday. I smelled a waft of leather and vanilla, and I knew who was standing at my office door. Eric.

I didn't look up; he didn't gesture or make a sound. Eric is attractive, and believe me, I see the signs. I'm not dumb, and while I can see myself enjoying him, I also know Eric's my boss, and getting involved with anyone I work with is not smart. Especially with William lurking around like a D1 hall monitor.

I was staring a hole into my desk calendar when Eric finally announced his presence.

"Morning, Ms. Reese," he said, taking one step over the threshold.

I looked up, faking surprise, "Eric, hi!" I exclaimed.

Today I was wearing Lark's royal blue strapless maxi dress, but I had a white button-up layered over it, tied at mid-waist. I followed Eric's eyes as I stood. He fought to keep them trained on mine, but they dipped to my hips, and by the small quiver in his smile, I could tell that in any other universe, he'd be ripping my clothes off. I won't lie, if William does succeed in getting me fired, I might just give Eric a go. I've been in an insane dry spell.

Eric continued his advance toward me and stopped when he was facing me, with only my desk between us. "I wanted to applaud your work with the St. Patty's Day luncheon. I had a lot of fun," he said while grabbing the hairs on the back of his neck and eyeing my row of picture frames on the shelf.

"Thank you!" I replied, still sitting, wondering if there was an underlying reason for this visit.

"You know, I'm actually half Irish," Eric disclosed, taking a seat in the chair across from me. He crossed his left leg over his right, and his pant leg rose, revealing maroon socks with little cookie prints. Does he have kids? He didn't strike me as a silly sock guy, not with all his suave mannerisms and charm.

"My mom is half Irish, along with a few other races," I retorted, laughing at my own joke.

"What about your dad?" he immediately replied, his interest at my sharing apparent.

"Same as my mom, not Irish, but mixed with a whole bunch. I'm fourth-generation multiracial. I don't think there's a race I'm not," I said, relaxing back into the chair.

"That's interesting, so you and your siblings do not identify as anything specific?" Eric said, leaning forward with inquiring lights dazzling in his dreamy eyes.

"No, never. I always tell a joke or something. I feel like if I claim one, I'm erasing the others," I said proudly.

"I like that," Eric clipped, leaning back into the chair. "What about your siblings?" he inquired, and I politely shrugged. We sat in silence for a beat, eyeing each other. Where William's eyes were dark, deep, serious, and restrained, Eric's eyes held something lighter—almost sparkling in a way your dog's do when you get home, or a kid's when gifted with a new toy. What am I thinking? Why is William even being compared to Eric? *Get your shit together, Wren.* I broke the silence. My voice came out raspy, and when I went to clear my throat, Eric spoke.

"I wanted to extend an invite to the company retreat this year. Usually, invites are sent via email in February, but you were freshly hired, so I don't believe you were on the list to receive one."

Instantly, I replied, "Oh! I'd love to come." I rose again and began putting my things into my bag, noting that the clock was half-past two. Busying myself in hopes he would take the hint.

"I'm working the rest of the day remotely, but please send me the details. My number is…" I began to tell him my phone number, and he stopped me.

"Oh, I already have it, and please feel free to bring your sisters." Eric replied, standing and walking me to my office door. I gave a tight smile and nodded.

When I got to the elevator, I rode it down alone. Thank God. The ride gave me a moment to clear my thoughts and refocus. All I could think about was how much I wanted to get home and take a nap. The exhaustion was catching up with me, and I needed a break from all the drama. The elevator dinged, and I stepped out, hoping the rest of the day would be uneventful enough to let me recharge.

Twelve

Mom's Birthday

Wren

March 20th

Today is Mom's birthday. Selah Reese, a Pisces, one of my favorite zodiac signs—though I might be biased since she is one. Pisces and Sagittarius are both mutable signs, which makes us compatible, or so they say. Astrology has always been Mom's thing. My mother has always been the go-with-the-flow type, very easygoing and adaptable. I think I inherited that from her, though I like to think I've added my own flair to it—a bit more sparkle, a bit more chaos.

I planned the best party for her. The snow disappeared a week ago, and we've been blessed with sunny weather this past week and today, clearing out the remnants of winter. The party's theme is 1950s chic.

The driveway is decorated like a drive-in burger stop, leading guests to walk through the "drive-in" to get to the backyard. Once in the back, there are black-and-white polka-dotted streamers hanging from trees and the surrounding white fence.

All the tables replicate pink poodle skirts with a white poodle being walked by a floating black leash. The plates are shaped like black vinyl records, and the drink station has little music notes floating in the cucumber water and spiked lemonade. Raven is helping me set up, even though she doesn't have an aesthetic bone in her body. Her outfit, though? Right on theme. She has her hair straightened and pulled back into a high ponytail of loose spiral curls. She has a front bang swooped back with pearl clips holding it in place. Raven's vintage polka dot halter cocktail dress is epic. She looks like she just stepped off a 1950s film set. While she's filling the pink mini Cadillacs on the food station with napkins, I'm using my emergency nail scissors to trim imperfections on the centerpieces. I'm so happy today is one of those rare warm pre-spring days; I could not have pulled this off inside the house.

I can be a bit of a perfectionist when it comes to details like this—I want everything to be just right, especially for Mom. There's something satisfying about seeing my vision come to life, each element fitting together perfectly, like a puzzle. I know it's a little extra, but I've always believed if you're going to do something, you might as well make it unforgettable. Besides, I love the look on people's faces when they see the final result. It makes all the late nights, the planning, and the obsessing worth it.

"Wow!" I hear the deep, familiar voice and turn to see my dad standing at the glass sliding doors that lead to the backyard. He's looking around, amazed at the transformation. I even had the pool covered with a dance floor. It was expensive, but I decided to dip into my savings a little—Mom is worth it. I smile when I realize he's dressed in theme: leather jacket, white tee tucked into jeans, and black-and-white oxfords. The photos from tonight will definitely be going in my portfolio.

"You really like it?" I ask nervously, looking around at the final product.

"Oh, Wren, you have outdone yourself. Wait until your mother sees this!" My dad side-hugs me with so much warmth and pride. I love my dad; he's always been a solid figure of support in my life. He's practical but open-minded, and some of the best advice I've ever gotten has come from him. Once I have kids, I have to ask him how he did it—raising four crazy girls without going insane himself.

"Thanks, Dad," I say with more appreciation than my voice can fully convey. Compliments are nice, but I always feel like they can't quite capture what I want them to. Still, I think Dad understands—he always does.

"Dad!" Raven yelps from behind us. We both turn to find Raven wobbling on a ladder. My dad runs to stabilize it while Raven descends. I shake my head, opting to walk into the kitchen instead of making a short joke at her expense. It's too easy at this point, but I know Raven's trying her best to help me out. Besides, teasing her too much today would just distract from the good vibes I'm trying to keep up.

Laughter fills the backyard, mingling with the sounds of chatter as Reese family and friends come together. However, one key player is missing—Mom. She's been lending a hand at Perch, Dove's bakery, completely unaware that the preparations she's helping with are for her own surprise party. Keeping Mom in the dark is no small feat; her intuition is sharp, and she's known to sniff out secrets like a bloodhound, so our best bet was to keep her occupied.

Surrounded by Raven, Lark, and my favorite twin cousins, Lorraine and Laura, I bask in the glow of their compliments about the epic party I've organized. The pride that swells within me is hard to contain. I can't help but beam at them, even as I try to play it cool. While I've thrown parties in the past, this event feels different, more personal, and their words of praise hit differently this time around. This party isn't just for show—it's for Mom, and I want her to feel all the love and effort we've poured into this.

Dad and his twin brother, Uncle Dame, stroll over, their banter adding to the festive vibe. We exchange smiles as Uncle Dame delivers a compliment to us all.

"You girls are looking flyyy," he exclaims.

"We aren't 'girls,' Dad," Lorraine quips with a playful eye roll.

"You'll always be my little girls," Uncle Dame teases, reaching over to affectionately pinch Lorraine and Laura's chins.

Growing up with twin dads has always been an adventure—they love to prank us and test our ability to tell them apart. While they've managed to sneak a few tricks past us, it's all in good fun. Lorraine and Laura feel more like additional sisters than cousins, often sleeping over in our prepubescent years. Over the years, my relationship with Laura has become strained because of a fight between her and Lark in college, but we're cordial enough to be around each other now. It doesn't mean

I don't sometimes wish things were different—I miss how close we used to be, but I've learned not everything can be fixed with a party or an apology.

A quiet excitement ripples through the backyard, drawing everyone's attention toward the front. As we make our way over, my phone buzzes with a text from Dove in our sister chat, adding an extra sprinkle of excitement to the already buzzing atmosphere.

Dove: 1) We're here. 2) Don't be weird!

As I begin to type out a response, confusion tugs at my mind. "Don't be weird?" What could she mean by that? Before I can delve deeper into the puzzling words, a commotion up ahead catches my attention. My gaze shifts, and in that moment, my mother steps into the scene, greeted by a resounding chorus of "SURPRISE!" from the guests. Startled, she clasps her heart before laughter bubbles forth as she surveys the scene around her. Despite not adhering to the party's theme, her casual attire of dark jeans and a light green blouse suits her perfectly, with her themed outfit awaiting her upstairs in her bedroom. Aunt Kat has also brought her styling supplies to work her magic on Mom's hair.

Seeing Mom's surprised face makes every bit of stress worth it—the late nights, the planning, the second-guessing. She's the type of person who does so much for everyone else without expecting anything in return, and today is her day to be celebrated. I want her to feel like a star.

"Oh my!" Mom exclaims as she receives hugs from various family members, finding solace in Dad's embrace. They have that timeless love that warms my heart, but the moment takes a turn when the affectionate peck on the lips escalates. Sensing the need for space, I shift my gaze to a trio approaching behind my mom. Dove is flanked by a tall, brawny redheaded man on her left—Doctor Bearclaw! Looks like Lark was right—and to his left stands…no, it couldn't be.

My sisters exchange a glance, questioning my obvious shock. The sight of William leaves my jaw figuratively and almost literally hitting the ground. With Mom escorted inside by Aunt Kat and Dad, the music fills the air, setting the vibrant ambiance for the ensuing festivities. Turning to face us, Dove conveys a silent plea for discretion, her eyes silently urging us to handle the situation with care.

I have to admit, one thing about me is that I don't always hide my feelings well—especially when I'm blindsided. And right now, I'm blindsided. It's like every nerve in my body is suddenly on high alert, my stomach twisting in knots at the sight of him.

"Nice to meet you all! Dove has been singing your praises," Marcus says, pulling us all into a hug. Releasing us from his embrace, my gaze darts to William, his calm demeanor irking me. How dare he attend my mother's birthday bash and act so nonchalant in my presence?

"This is my best friend, Will…" Marcus begins, but I quickly interject, "William," emphasizing each syllable.

Silence hangs in the air, all eyes turning to focus on me. Refusing to back down, I continue, "We work together, at least until he successfully gets me fired. Right, Will?" I sarcastically chuckle. Tension crackles between us as our stares lock, his unwavering coolness a stark contrast to my simmering frustration. Clad in a blue and white letterman jacket with a fitted white tee and jeans, he exudes a laid-back charm, and I want to smack that blank stare right off his face.

Sometimes, I know I can be a bit too much—too intense, too passionate, too unwilling to let things slide. But I don't care right now. This is my mom's day, and I'll be damned if anyone, especially William, thinks they can just show up and ruin my vibe.

"It was a pleasure meeting you, Marcus. Enjoy the party," I say with a polite smile, straightening my posture and lifting my chin before briskly turning on my heels, intent on putting some distance between myself and my newfound shadow, William. There's a difference between letting things go with the flow and letting someone walk all over you—and today, I'm drawing that line.

Thirteen

Party Continues

Wren

March 20th

I watch as my mom re-enters the party, a vision of elegance and charm with her beautifully styled hair and stunning outfit. Her red lips are accentuated with a touch of vintage glamour, and the small cat-eye winged liner adds a playful yet sophisticated edge to her look. Dressed in a flowing red cocktail dress that drapes gracefully over her tan shoulders, she radiates timeless beauty. The pearls sitting around her neck serve as the perfect finishing touch, completing her ensemble.

The festivities unfold around me, the party buzzing with energy and laughter as guests mingle and celebrate. I catch snippets of well-wishes for my mom's birthday and see a flurry of attention around Dove, where nosy family members eagerly seek an introduction to Marcus. I can't help but smile at the thought of teasing my sister like any little sister would—it's practically my job description—but the prospect of crossing paths with William hovers above, like an unwelcome cloud threatening to rain on my good time.

I make my way towards the DJ booth, a plate of food and a cold drink in hand as a small offering of appreciation. The tension in the air pricks at my senses, a burnt tinge that lingers around me as I sense his gaze on me. Ugh, why does he have to do that? With a nonchalant glance around the party—because, of course, I'm too cool to acknowledge the unease—I seek out the familiar figure of William—his broad shoulders and intense brown eyes standing out among the crowd. I spot him standing with Marcus and my cousins Anthony and June, the twins who always bring weed to our events. Twins, it seems, run strongly in our family; we have at least two sets every generation. It's honestly ridiculous—like, how do we always end up with double trouble?

"Hey, I brought you a plate and some cucumber water. I haven't seen you drink anything since arriving," I chirp cheerfully, setting down the refreshments in an empty spot near the DJ booth. I'm practically the patron saint of DJs tonight—someone should give me a medal.

The DJ, who goes by the name KP, glances up at me with a warm smile, a single headphone perched between his shoulder and ear. "Thanks, I didn't even realize," he replies, his charm evident in the curve of his lips as he gratefully accepts the drink. Returning his smile, I share a knowing nod. "I work in the party industry, so I know how quickly you can forget to drink or eat at an event." Trust me, been there, starved that.

As KP hits a button on his laptop and removes his headphones completely, I take a step up onto the platform he's stationed on. He takes a sip of the drink, finishing it in one gulp, and his gaze lingers on me as he smiles once more. Curiosity piqued, he inquires about my work, prompting me to share snippets of my current job, my aspirations, and even the ongoing workplace drama with a certain individual attempting to sabotage my standing. (Hi, William. No, I'm not talking about you… okay, I totally am.) The candid flow of conversation offers a welcome distraction.

As I ramble on, immersed in the comforting exchange of stories and personal insight, KP's genuine interest in my tales instills a sense of ease in me. Suddenly, a weight presses down on my shoulder from behind, and a jolt of surprise courses through me. Turning on my heel, I face William, who stands with an air of calm that belies the unspoken currents simmering beneath his façade. His eyes, usually a mask of impassivity, betray a flicker of emotion that raises a sliver of interest within me. Meeting his gaze with trepidation, I lock eyes with him, the elevation of the DJ booth giving me a slight advantage as I peer down at him. William's gaze flits behind me briefly before returning to meet mine, his usual composure tinged with a note of hesitancy.

"Let's talk." The request hangs in the air, and I turn, looking behind me just to escape his glare, and exhale quickly. Ugh, why now? Can't we just pretend everything is fine for one night?

"Why?" I challenge, my voice laced with skepticism. William's steady gaze remains fixed on me, his brows knitting together in contemplation before he finally responds with characteristic dryness, "To clarify things."

An eye roll escapes me, a gesture that doesn't go unnoticed as I step down from the DJ booth, gesturing towards a quieter corner of the yard, away from the party's bustling throng. As we part through the crowd, the scrutinizing glances and devilish smiles from my sisters offer a silent commentary on the awkward scene playing out before them. I swear, my sisters live for my drama. As we round the corner of the house, the rolling tension between us thickens. William stands before me, arms crossed, feet planted shoulder-width apart, a slow smirk growing. Oh great, here comes Mr. Broody.

"I did not know this would be your mother's party. Marcus invited me for support…" William begins, his words layered with an unmistakable hint of remorse. I attempt to process his vague explanation, though the sight of his arms folded over his chest only serves to emphasize the solidity of his presence, distracting me from his words. I cross my arms to mirror his posture, which boosts my chest, and it does not go unnoticed. His features soften ever so slightly, his arms loosening their grip but still crossed against his chest.

Nodding in acknowledgment, I consider turning to leave, eager to evade this conversation painted with discomfort. Before I can make a move, a familiar hand settles on my shoulder once more, halting my retreat. Fixing my gaze on him, I'm met with a storm of emotions swirling in his eyes.

"Why are you like this?" William questions, an undercurrent of exasperation coloring his tone. He releases his arms, and they sit upon his hips, like a principal reprimanding a student. Oh, great, I'm getting the "why are you like this" talk now? Fabulous. Surprised by the accusation, I meet his gaze with a spark of defiance.

"Me?" I counter, disbelief coloring my response. I point at my chest, eyes roaming in literal search of an answer. Seriously, have you met me? I'm adorable!

"Yes, you. You're infuriating," he huffs, the lines of his face softening as he runs a hand over his short hair. His admission takes me aback, confusion and anger pooling within me.

"What? Have you met yourself? It's all broody, silent, sexy 'I'm Batman' vibes with you. Chill out!" I retort, using my best Batman voice at the perfect peak of the statement. A grin starts tugging at the corners of my lips despite the brewing tension between us, and my hand flies over my mouth to hide the small smile and ghost of a chuckle that follows. I can't help it; I happen to be one of those people who laugh at their own jokes—somebody has to!

His chuckle in response only fans the flames of my exasperation. However, just as I turn to walk away, he spins me back around completely, catching me off balance. A grin lingers on his lips, a glint of mischief in his eyes. Facing him, boxed in by his proximity, I feel the cool brick of the house against my back and the warmth of William's body at my front. The shift in his demeanor sends a shiver down my spine, his voice lowering to a hypnotic timbre that erodes my resolve. His lips ghosting against my neck sparks a rush of sensation, a wave of desire that threatens to overwhelm me.

"Don't..." he whispers, breaths away from my ear.

As our eyes meet, a fleeting moment of vulnerability flickers in his gaze, revealing a depth of passion and restraint that tugs at my insides. The anticipation hangs heavy in the air, the promise of a forbidden moment that lingers just out of reach. In that suspended moment, as the space between us narrows to nothing, the air becoming thicker and the heat between us boiling, I close my eyes in silent surrender, the breath of possibility tingling against my skin. But as quickly as the tension builds, it dissipates, replaced by a cold emptiness that trails in his wake. I feel him pull away before I open my eyes to confirm.

The mask returns to its place, the walls closing off whatever vulnerability had shone through. William, bottled right back up. I shake my head in disbelief, laughter bubbling up as I pat him on the shoulder and squeeze by him, the echoes of our almost-kiss lingering in the air like a forbidden melody. Seriously, why are boys so confusing?

* * *

William

From a table in the corner of the yard, I switch from conversing with Marcus and Dove to Wren's cousins to watching Wren again. As she flits between conversations, her every gesture and expression radiates effortless charm. A flicker of jealousy stirs within me. The sight of her drifting towards the DJ with a plate and cup in hand sends a wave of heat through my chest—an overwhelming possessiveness that threatens to overrun my senses. I feel a primal, almost violent urge to drag her away from anyone who might steal her attention, a battle between the yearning to claim her and the need to maintain a fragile facade of detachment.

The urge is suffocating, my fists clenching involuntarily as I watch her smile at the DJ. Driven by a volatile blend of envy and impulse, I yield to my instincts. I push forward, interrupting her conversation. She hesitates, eyes narrowing, but eventually agrees to talk. I have no plan, no clever words to charm her. I just need her with me, need to keep her from slipping away. Once we make it to the side of the house, away from the rumble of the party, the silence between us stretches taut, every thread tightening until it feels like we might snap. We end up arguing, of course—it's the only thing we seem capable of.

"I did not know this would be your mother's party," I start as we settle on the side of the house. My arms fold over my chest, my muscles tense, as if trying to shield myself from the intensity of her glare.

She looks to the side, her jaw tight, as if contemplating leaving, and something inside me snaps. My emotions bubble over, rage and desperation mingling until I can't hold back. I grab her shoulders, not gently, and lean down, my eyes boring into hers. Anything to keep her here, to keep her focused on me.

"Why are you like this?" I blurt out, my voice raw, almost a growl, more to myself than to her, my frustration spilling over.

"Me?" Wren exclaims, her eyes blazing, the fire in her stare matching my own.

"Yes, you, you're infuriating," I reply, my voice harsh, every word edged with a desperation I can't hide.

"What? Have you met yourself? It's all broody, sexy 'I'm Batman' vibes with you. Chill out!" she yells back, her anger clashing with mine. But then, despite the fury in her eyes, her lips quirk into a sly grin, and she lets out a small laugh. That sound—that beautiful sound—hits me like a punch to the gut. I need to hear it again. My own grin breaks free, a rare crack in my defenses, and for a moment, I want nothing more than to live in this fragile reality, to forget everything else.

But Wren breaks away, turning to leave, and before I know it, my hand is on her arm, stopping her. The energy between us shifts, something dark and electric crackling in the air. The tension is almost unbearable, the hunger in her gaze mirroring my own. Her lips part slightly, a subtle invitation, and all I can think about is how much I want her—how much I need her.

I hover on the edge of surrender, my resolve hanging by a thread. The brute force of my desire, the need to claim her, to make her mine, surges through me. My chest heaves, every breath a struggle against the urge to pull her against me and take what I want. I am so close to giving in, to letting everything else fall away, to losing myself in her. But somewhere, deep in the haze of my need, a fragment of reason holds me back. I can't do this—I can't cross this line. Not with her. Not like this.

With a guttural growl, I force myself to step back, my hands dropping to my sides. The tension between us lingers, thick and heavy, but I turn away, every muscle in my body screaming in protest. I have to protect her in some way, even if that means protecting her from myself. If denying myself is the only way to do that, then I will wield that weapon with all the strength I have left.

* * *

Wren

Margaritas are being made inside while they interrogate Dove and me. Lark is cutting lemons and limes, Raven is adding tequila to the blender, and Dove is sitting on the stool next to me, swaying back and forth.

"Marcus, huh?" Lark says, winking at me. Guess she was right. Want something found out? Forget the FBI, call Lark. Dove responds with a shy smile. We all look at her, and because I'm trying to stay out of the hot seat, I jump on the bandwagon of inquisition.

"When did you guys meet?" I turn and ask Dove. Her eyes widen just a little in disbelief that I'm the first to shoot. I send a pleading look her way, and her brows relax.

"January. I told him about Mom's party, and he wanted to come. He invited his friend to make it less weird," she replies nonchalantly.

"Yeah, right, LESS weird," Lark retorts, using air quotes and dropping a lime to the floor.

I stand and remove the frozen strawberries from the freezer, handing them to Raven, who is using the drink booklet Mom got at Costco. Of course, Raven can't even make drinks without following the instructions.

"So, that's William," Raven says, looking up at me, smirking. "I see why he has your panties in such a bunch now." She continues. Pressing the high-speed button on the blender to avoid Raven's question, the kitchen fills with the harsh noises of ice being crushed. "Don't. Start," I say, wiping my face in embarrassment and walking back to my stool.

"Oh, come on, Wren. You know we're all curious," Lark chimes in, a teasing grin on her face. "You're usually an open book. What's the deal with this guy?" She arches an eyebrow, clearly enjoying my discomfort. I roll my eyes in response, trying to ignore the heat creeping up my cheeks.

"It's nothing," I mumble, but my sisters know better. They can read me like a children's bedtime story. Lark gives me an exaggerated, knowing nod, and Raven snorts in amusement.

I look out the glass sliding doors to the backyard and see William standing by my dad at the grill. They're talking animatedly with their hands and laughing. I didn't think William could look so free and at ease, but then I remember him smiling with the brunette at the diner and then the bistro. Who was that woman? He was also laughing with Marcus prior to fetching me from the DJ booth. So what about me prompts him to bestow half-smiles and hard stares? I watch as Uncle Dame joins them, and the laughter and camaraderie heighten. My uncle pats William on the back, hands him a beer, and I think I might be in the wrong reality.

"Hello!" all three of my sisters say in unison as Dove pokes me. I snap back to our conversation, and Dove recounts the few details she's comfortable sharing about her new relationship. I stay clear of mentioning William, and when the margaritas are done, we dress the glasses with sugar and lime. One red serving tray of strawberry margaritas in hand, we all head back outside. The party is nearing the end, and the early spring weather is bringing in a crisp night air. The older family members are beginning to trickle out, leaving the younger adult cousins to enjoy playing cards and drinking without censorship.

The evening stretches on as the clock ticks towards midnight, leaving only a handful of family members lingering around the long table. The surrounding back patio is heated, giving us some warmth in the night breeze. My parents have retreated inside to watch their favorite show, leaving the rest of us engrossed in an unforgiving game of spades. Lorraine, my partner in crime for the game, sits across from me as we eye-signal our next move. Further down the table, Anthony and Raven, who were soundly defeated by William and Marcus, sit in good humor, cheering on their victors.

"How do you even know how to play spades?" Laura, my cousin, directs her question at Marcus, curiosity lacing her tone.

"Will taught me. He's really good at it!" Marcus replies with a proud grin as he slaps a hard hand on William's shoulder. The spotlight shifts, and all eyes turn to William, who sits stoically next to Laura.

"I'm good with numbers. If you pay attention well enough, the numbers tell you what's next," he explains with calm confidence.

"So, you count cards?" Anthony bursts out with exuberance, a mischievous spark lighting up his eyes. "We're going to Vegas, man!" he exclaims, standing and slapping William in the same spot as Marcus, eliciting a chuckle from the group. William releases a brief shy smile, the first window I've caught into a different side of him.

"You could say that, but I'm not allowed in Vegas," William responds nonchalantly, a hint of amusement underlying his words. The revelation hangs in the air like a sudden twist in the game, drawing the attention of everyone at the table. Lark leans forward, her eyes wide with curiosity as she broaches the burning question on everyone's mind.

"Why are you not allowed in Vegas, William?" she prompts, the anticipation bubbling in the silenced atmosphere. William meets her gaze with a grin, his eyes twinkling with a hint of mischief.

"Counting cards," he quips, plucking a spade from his hand and slamming it onto the table to seal the win for his team, inciting a chorus of laughter and light banter around the table. I throw my remaining cards down and pull my hoodie closer to my chin.

"Classic Wren," Lark whispers to me. "Always trying to keep it cool, but inside, I know you're freaking out right now." She flashes me a playful grin, and I can't help but laugh.

"You wish," I reply, trying to sound confident, but I know she's right. There's something about William that has my thoughts running in circles, and my sisters know it. They always do.

My attention shifts to William. The tale of his Vegas banishment strikes me as unexpected and oddly intriguing. As every layer unravels, he perplexes me further. Maybe, if I just keep peeling, who knows what might be in there. His coffee-colored eyes meet mine before I can look away, locking in an unspoken exchange that aches in the silent spaces between us. The sounds of conversation fade into the background, replaced by an exchange that sends me aback.

"Ooh, the tension," Raven whispers, nudging Lark. I can feel my cheeks heat up again. "Wren, if you stare any harder, he might just combust," she adds with a laugh.

"Shut up," I mutter, pulling my hoodie strings tighter around my face in a poor attempt to hide. Raven just giggles, clearly delighted by my discomfort.

A smile graces his lips, and like a strike of lightning to the chest, I feel a spark. Torn between curiosity, anger, and an unspoken attraction, I tear my gaze away, seeking solace in the familiar faces around the table. Dove's knowing gaze meets mine, a silent acknowledgment passing between us. She softens her face like she's asking a question through our sister connection:

Are you okay?

"You're really gonna leave us hanging, Wren?" Lark asks, her voice filled with faux outrage. "The night is still young!"

Sensing the weight of the liquor I consumed tonight, the roller coaster of emotion William provides, and the lack of sleep preparing for the party, I continue to rise from my seat, announcing my departure for the night. A wave of disappointment ripples through the group. Like a hawk, William's gaze pierces through the crowd, a silent challenge that stirs a mix of defiance within me. Ignoring the lingering tension and the silent demand, I collect my empty bottles, toss them into the recycling bin, and bid everyone goodnight.

"We're not done with you yet, Wren!" Lark calls after me, her laughter following me inside. I smile to myself, shaking my head. My sisters never let anything slide, and I wouldn't have it any other way. Heading to my room, I can't help but think about everything that happened tonight—the laughter, the tension, and William's mysterious charm. Tomorrow, I know I'll have to face the questions I've been avoiding, but for now, I let the warmth of the night settle over me, ready to see what the morning brings.

Fourteen

Rick & Morty

William

March 26th

Today is a departure from my norm—I'm running late for work, hungover from a dream too vivid to recount; Wren's body tangled in my sheets and me above her. Hurrying through the lobby, I weave through the bustling space with a sense of urgency, intent on catching the closing elevator before it slips out of reach. The golden doors are nearly closed when an unexpected interruption—a midair binder— swiftly halts their descent, granting me entrance into the awaiting box.

And there she stands, a bewitching mirage made flesh, leaning against the back wall of the elevator, head held high. Her legs are elegantly crossed at the ankle, her heels offering a glimpse of toes painted with pristine white polish, a contrast against the soft, ethereal pink of her dress. I steady myself and step into the elevator, the air thick and uncomfortable.

"Thank you," I offer, a feeble attempt to break the silence that hangs between us in the confined space.

"No problemo," she responds casually, but with a slight furrow of her brows.

"Are you okay?" I inquire as we ascend, a note of concern seeping into my tone.

"Yeah, I don't know why I said that. I never say that." She scratches her elbow and then straightens, releasing a small nervous laugh. As the silence thickens, a sense of unease settles over us, prompting me to fill the void with idle conversation. "Jerry Smith is excited for National Pet Day," I offer, a poor attempt to bridge the growing silence.

"Oh wow, really? I wasn't sure if you were bringing him," she responds, accompanied by a fleeting glance in my direction, a subtle invitation to engage. I offer no response, the weight of her gaze lingering on me as the elevator reaches its destination, the doors sliding open to reveal the seventh floor. Stepping onto solid ground, she offers a parting grin and a casual farewell, "See ya later, Rick."

Misinterpreting her goodbye, I turn my head in confusion until the realization hits me like a bolt of lightning—her reference is to Rick & Morty, and my dog's name being inspired by the show. A tingling grows in my chest, a surprising smirk gracing my lips as I grasp the hidden meaning behind her words. Twice, Wren has left me grinning in this damn elevator.

* * *

Seated at my desk, the soft glow of the desk lamp casts a warm light over the clutter of papers and folders before me. I find myself lost in a sea of financial statements that seem to blur into an incomprehensible mess. The files for a new account I pulled last minute lay open, their contents a jumbled maze of numbers and figures that refuse to yield their secrets. Frustration mounts within me as I close my laptop with a heavy sigh, removing my glasses and running a hand over my tired eyes.

While my career has always been a source of passion and fulfillment, today a shadow of doubt begins to creep in, its tendrils winding their way through the cracks in my carefully constructed facade. I've worked diligently to reach this position at such a young age, the path to success paved with dedication and countless sacrifices. Yet, as I sit contemplating the future that stretches out before me, a nagging question lingers in my mind: Will this be the sum of my existence, a relentless cycle of work and corporate advancement?

The image of her dances unbidden into my thoughts, the memories of our shared moments vivid and alive in my mind. She appears before me in the red dress she wore at the Valentine's Day party, twirling amidst a garden of vibrant blooms, her laughter a melody that fills the silent spaces of my fantasy. A rare glimpse of my unrestrained self emerges, a full untamed smile gracing my lips as I bask in the warmth of her presence. Her playful smirk beckons me closer, a silent invitation that I accept, joining behind her as she sways against me.

In my dream, I take another step towards her, drawn inexorably by the magnetic pull of her. Yet, with each stride I take, she recedes further and further, a teasing mirage that slips beyond my grasp. A sense of urgency grips me, my smile fading into a furrow as I quicken my pace to close the widening gap between us. Just as I am on the brink of reaching her, the jarring ping of an email alert disrupts the reverie, jolting me back to the stark reality of my office surroundings, the distant echoes of her laughter fading into the ether.

The screen of my laptop illuminates with an email notification, the sender's name—Shiva—causing a twinge of pain to cross my chest as I read it. It's a reminder about the impromptu board meeting scheduled. With every confirmation of attendance from the board members, my stomach curls with whispers of indecision. The weight of expectation bears down on me, a heavy burden to prove my worth among peers who may not fully comprehend the depths of my dedication. As I grapple with these conflicting scenarios and possibilities, a fierce resolve settles within me, a determination to show the board my indispensable value to the firm.

Eric, born into privilege and handed his career on a silver platter by his father, seems to navigate life with an effortless energy that eludes me. I carry the weight of my working-class roots and the sacrifices made along the way to secure a brighter future. The path to success has been paved with late nights, exhausting jobs, unwavering dedication, and a relentless pursuit of excellence that has defined my journey thus far. The recent hiring of Wren, a decision that Eric made without due consideration, leaves me with a terrible choice, and all the more reason to dislike him. I genuinely like Wren, but my hands are tied; gunning for her job and her heart feels a bit overkill on the villain spectrum. With a shake of my head, I try to banish the self-deprecating thoughts, turning my focus to the glowing screen of the company messenger app. My fingers glide across the keyboard, hesitating over her name before finally initiating a new thread. Staring at the blank entry box, my hands hover over the keyboard.

After a moment of hesitation, I compose a message with an air of nonchalance:

William Jones: Wubba Lubba Dub Dub

The message hangs in the digital ether, and my mind begins to unravel the many reasons she's already blocked me. Regret floods in as I read the words back to myself, a pang of embarrassment surging through me. She likely won't understand the reference, leaving me feeling like a fool for attempting such a cryptic message. I lean back in my chair, spinning to look out the window, as the sea of buildings grants no relief. The agonizing pause stretches on, punctuated only by the mocking presence of the three dots indicating her typing. Frustrated with my own lack of restraint, I swiftly exit the messenger app, electing to bury myself in the comforting monotony of financial statements for the Beck account.

A sudden ping alerts me to a new message. With a swift intake of breath, I click back to the messenger app in a flurry of movement, curiosity and trepidation warring within me as I read her response.

Wren Reese: Oh Geez!!

The message lingers on the screen before me, a nod to the shared reference. I return to the documents before me for a moment to calm my excitement at our shared joke, and time drifts by, slipping through my grasp like sand, until the rumble of my stomach begs for lunch. My elbow hits the mouse while standing, and the messaging thread between Wren and me illuminates on my computer screen. I slouch back into my seat, remembering the reason for my grand mood shift. I want to ask her to lunch; I could show her my favorite cheeseburger spot, a place I proficiently gate-keep, but I don't ask. I have to save her job first, at least. A sense of resignation settles over me as I push back from my desk, the messenger app still open but untouched. With a heavy sigh, I rise from my seat and make my way towards the lunch crowd, abandoning the thread.

Fifteen

Closeted

William

April 11th

National Pet Day has arrived, and the office is saturated with the scent of animals, filled to the brim with furry companions of all shapes and sizes. The midday celebration is taking place on the 5th floor, due to its temporary vacancy before renovations begin next quarter, and I couldn't be happier. I definitely wouldn't want my floor to smell as bad as the elevator does today. Despite my lingering doubts about the wisdom of the event, as Jerry Smith playfully wags his tail and brushes against my leg, a rare smile graces my face. I hadn't anticipated how comforting it would be to have him by my side at the office. While he isn't officially an emotional support animal, Jerry Smith seems to understand my unspoken cues when anxiety or contemplation clouds my thoughts. It's both amusing and humbling to acknowledge that my dog possesses more emotional awareness than I do.

I step off the elevator onto the 5th floor, surrounded by a burst of reds and dark purples, as a cacophony of barks and meows meets my ears. Most of the animals are on leashes, but a few roam freely, including a lizard perched on Killian's shoulder—the IT guy who only appears in the office when someone clicks a suspicious email link. Wary of the chaotic crowd, I loop Jerry Smith's leash around my hand twice, creating a sense of control as he instinctively settles at my feet, attuned to my subtle signals. A Welsh Corgi with a tannish-gray coat and a white belly, I adopted him years ago at a farmer's market, guided by an impulsive decision to bring home the runt of the litter. From that fateful day, Jerry Smith became my best friend, jokingly named after a character he whined like as a pup. To this day, we still watch *Rick & Morty* together.

Observing Jerry Smith's inquisitive gaze drifting towards an incoming ball, I follow his line of sight to see Wren approaching, her radiant smile and friendly wave sending a golden jolt of nerves through me and my dog. The previous exchange on the messaging app pops into the forefront of my mind, leaving me questioning the appropriate demeanor to adopt in her presence. Should I exhibit friendliness, maintain a courteous distance, or simply act natural? What would be natural exactly? With each step she takes, my inner turmoil intensifies.

"Oh, what an adorable little guy!" Wren exclaims as she draws near, dropping down to rub Jerry Smith's head, eliciting his playful display of rolling onto his back to expose his belly. Quite the charmer, that one.

"Jerry seems quite content," she remarks, her wide brown-green eyes sparkling with delight. Some days, her eyes gleam like vibrant emeralds with a hint of brown at the outer rims, while on other occasions, like today, the earthy brown hues seem to dominate, creating a mesmerizing blend of tones that stand out against her deep olive complexion. It's a sight that never fails to captivate me; indeed, it has become my favorite color.

"Jerry Smith," I respond, the words emerging flatly from my mouth, prompting me to offer a slight smile to soften the blunt delivery.

"Oh, my apologies! Jerry SMITH," Wren corrects herself with a chuckle, exchanging playful banter with Jerry Smith before showering him with affection. As she greets him with warmth and laughter, he reciprocates by affectionately licking her nose. Jerry Smith's unusually rapid comfort with Wren is keenly noticeable, even for a perceptive dog like him. However, my attention is diverted as a brown Labrador eagerly joins the duo, nudging his head between Wren's legs in a sign of familiarity. Without missing a beat, Wren leans down to reciprocate the gesture, planting a gentle kiss on the Lab's head, her natural ease in the company of animals giving me one more reason for my obsession.

"This sweet lady is Grizzly," she says, standing up and wiping off her dark-colored jeans that fit her in all the right places. I try not to, but my eyes fall to her hips for a moment, and I begin to spiral. I save myself by throwing out the only thought my mind can produce.

"I didn't know you had a dog," I say, grabbing at the back of my neck.

"Oh, she isn't mine. Grizzly is Dove's dog. She spends a lot of time at my parents' house because of the bakery's busy seasons," she replies.

"My sister Lark is here too—she's over there helping," Wren continues. I just nod and look in the direction she pointed. Near the goodie bag table is Lark's tall, lean figure straightening a centerpiece that looks to be a giant dog bone with a bow on top. She looks up and waves, and I politely wave back.

"It's nice she could come and assist," I say, searching for anything to prolong our contact.

"Yeah, with all the pets, I knew I'd need an extra hand," she mentions, her fingers restlessly toying with the denim fabric of her jeans. Does she feel the same nervousness in my presence that I do in hers? It seems unlikely. Wren is a force of nature, a ball of energy and confidence that rarely falters. Dismissing the thought, I politely excuse myself, feeling the weight of tension hanging between us as I make my way towards the gated play area with Jerry Smith.

Wren and Lark are chatting and laughing by the food setup, while Eric catches my eye as he talks with Maurice across the room, his gaze shifting towards Wren and Lark, a knowing smile playing on his lips. The room fills with the sounds of barking dogs, and soon, Jerry Smith makes his way over to me, his tail wagging excitedly before he darts off into the gated play area. What starts as innocent play soon escalates into a rambunctious tussle between a terrier and a poodle, setting off a chain reaction of barks and growls from the onlooking canines. As owners intervene to calm the chaos, a few guests scurry for the exit with their pets in hand.

With the energy of the party beginning to ebb, I join the efforts to clean up, grabbing a garbage bag from Lark as she busies herself dismantling the event setup. Jerry Smith lounges nearby, content in his own world, playing with the hem of a tablecloth. However, as minutes pass and Wren remains missing, a sense of unease tugs at me, prompting a quiet search. Following the soft sounds of muffled cries, I'm drawn to a darkened closet in the back of the room. Upon opening the door, a faint outline of Wren atop a stack of printer-paper-filled boxes catches my eye. Her silent tears and pained sounds tug at my heartstrings, filling me with an overwhelming rage—whoever made her cry would pay.

Taking a deep breath, I approach her tentatively, crouching down to meet her eye level with a gentle yet concerned gaze. "Hey, are you alright?"

* * *

Wren

Tears stream down my cheeks, my emotions climbing past my wall of detachment as I find solace in the storage closet. The event, despite not being a catastrophic failure, feels like the final straw today—the weight that has finally broken me. It's all just too much to process right now. The constant tightrope walk on the edge of employment adds to the overwhelming sense of pressure crushing down on me. And then there's Josh.

Josh, my ex-boyfriend, whose unexpected call this morning has unearthed a door of unresolved emotions and regrets. I thought he had moved on. His initial attempts to reach out dwindled, and I deluded myself into thinking that perhaps closure had nestled into the crevices of our fractured relationship. But his sudden call today, his request to meet face to face, reignited a forgotten anxiety within me. Yet, my cowardice—my inability to confront the realities I've long neglected—won out, and I declined his invitation, only to be met with a barrage of chastisement and condescension. His words cut deep, pulling at the insecurities I've grappled with in the shadows of my own self-doubt.

Josh said I was still acting like a "child running from adult responsibilities" and that planning parties with my degrees was an insult to my education. I wanted to shout, to tell him how wrong he was! But was he? The events of today, the disarray of the party I poured my heart into, added fuel to the fire. The chaos that unfolded—the dogs erupting into a violent scuffle, the shock and dismay on the faces of the guests as they fled—painted a grand picture of my failure. As I moved to intervene in the scuffle, my vision blurred, and my heart began beating so loudly I could no longer hear the barks. The burden of it all began to weigh me down. I tasted the salt of tears welling in my eyes, and the air in my lungs grew thick. With a heavy heart and leaden footsteps, I sought refuge in the storage closet.

I don't hear anyone enter, but I sense the shift in the atmosphere—a subtle change that triggers the sensation of someone's presence. With my hands shielding my tear-streaked face, I brace myself for the inevitable interruption, mistakenly assuming it to be Lark.

"Are you alright?" His voice is soft and concerned. The urge to lift my gaze and meet William's eyes tugs at me, but the fear of vulnerability, of exposing my fragile state to his critical gaze, holds me back. In this moment, breaking down at work feels like a betrayal of the facade I've meticulously crafted.

"I just need to be alone," I reply, the words quivering—a weak attempt to maintain a semblance of composure. William's muted acknowledgment punctuates the silence that descends, a heavy blanket draping over us in the confines of the dimly lit closet. As I slowly lower my hands from my face, the shadows of the closet envelop me, my senses sharpening to the darkness. I can feel William's fixed gaze upon me.

"We can be alone together," his words crack through my armor like a sword to the plate.

Sixteen

Lunch On Me

William

April 13th

Returning to my task of drafting agreements for the Beck account, the tranquility is broken by a notification from the company-wide messenger app. The message that flashes on the screen catches me off guard:

Wren Reese: I want to take you to lunch. Be ready @ 2 :)

A surge of adrenaline courses through me at the unexpected invitation. A faint smile graces my lips as thoughts race through my mind, contemplating the reasons behind Wren's sudden offer. Could it be a chance to address the unresolved tension from our last meeting in the closet?

I reply:

**William Jones: Carl's at 12p on Ferry Street / meet you in the
lobby**

She hearted the message. No reply.

** * **

Two hours later, punctuality being a virtue close to my heart, I find
myself waiting in the lobby precisely at 11:58 a.m. Glancing down at
my favorite watch—the first big purchase after law school, a prized
possession that reflects my commitment to timeliness—I watch as a
pair of sneakers comes into view, halting just inches away from me.
Following the trail upwards, my eyes trace the journey from white
Converse-clad feet to the figure of Wren standing before me. Her
punctual entrance, a rarity in my experience, prompts a flicker of
satisfaction. Most women I've encountered in similar circumstances
are known for their habitual tardiness, making her timely arrival a
refreshing change.

"Why are you looking at me like that?" Wren's voice interrupts my
thoughts, her head cocked to the side inquisitively.

My mental smile slips onto my face before I can stop it. "You're on
time," I respond, the remark slipping out before I can filter it through
my brooding facade.

"Well, it's only proper not to keep someone waiting," Wren replies, a casual sweep of her curls punctuating her response.

"You wore sneakers with that?" I question, my gaze drifting from her elegant black dress with a daring slit neckline to her choice of footwear. Wren's genuine laughter fills the space between us.

"Well, you mentioned Carl's, and that's a bit of a hike in heels, so I opted for my emergency shoes. Hence, the Chucks," Wren explains, gesturing towards her footwear with a playful flourish. My lack of foresight regarding the walk to Carl's dawns on me—the distance was intentional, not wanting to run into another coworker—but I hadn't considered she'd be dressed for the office.

"Practical choice," I acknowledge, holding the lobby door open as a silent invitation for Wren to walk ahead. A light touch at the small of her back guides her forward, prompting a subtle reaction, a shiver barely discernible beneath my fingertips.

* * *

We embark on the walk to Carl's in comfortable silence, Wren absorbing the surroundings with a tourist's curiosity, her eyes flitting from one point of interest to another. Curiosity gets the better of me, prompting me to inquire if she's a recent arrival to the area, only to learn that she has spent her entire life here. As we come to a stop outside the restaurant, I halt before the door, and a flicker of hesitation follows in her step. With a wave of bold action, I extend my hand, delicately resting it on her stomach—a tender gesture that pauses her movement. As she instinctively stays in place, watching me with those wide, emerald eyes, I seize the opportunity to open the door with a silent flourish of chivalry. Stepping back, I guide her forward, and before she can extinguish that beautiful smile, I drink in every bit of it.

* * *

Seated at Carl's, the ambiance shifts to a cozy booth. Wren slides towards the very end of the table, the subtle invitation for closer proximity hanging in the air. Opting for caution, I settle across from her. My gaze roams from the delicate curve of her neck to the subtle arch of her cheekbones, and the gentle sweep of her lips, perpetually curved in a smile. As the moment lingers, our eyes meet, the unexpected connection breaking the spell that holds me captive. With a subtle clearing of my throat, the trance is lifted, and reality reasserts itself.

"Do you want anything to drink, sir?" the host inquires.

"Water is fine," I reply, my fingers instinctively loosening my tie as I shift uneasily in my seat. Following the host's exit, a new presence graces our table—the server, who places napkins before us with practiced ease.

"Hi, my name is Kelly, welcome to Carl's. I will be your server today. Can I start you two off with some drinks from the bar or our new beer-battered string beans?"

"Hi Kelly! I'm Wren. Miranda, the host, already took our drink orders, but as for food, we haven't had much time to look over the menu. Can you give us—"

"We'll take two cheeseburgers, medium well," I interject.

"Oh, well, can you add mustard to mine?" Wren's eyes flit between me and Kelly, a hint of mischief dancing in her gaze.

"Sure thing, hun," Kelly responds before gliding off to attend to other patrons. In the pause that follows, our eyes meet in a silent exchange. Folding my hands on the table, I attempt a straight face before leaning in towards Wren, ready to deliver a playful jab.

"Wren, mustard on a cheeseburger has to be a crime."

Momentarily taken aback, she transforms her gaze to amusement, her expression meeting my unexpected display of humor. "Oh, boo-hoo, everyone hates that I like mustard. To be honest, at this point, I'm sure people don't really hate it. Ketchup started a smear campaign and paid people to comply," Wren quips with a twinkle in her eyes.

As her words hang in the air, I can't stifle the deep, genuine laugh that comes forth. Her wit and humor are a breath of fresh air.

"Oh my god. You laugh?" she exclaims, her smile spreading further across her face.

"I'm human, aren't I?" I answer.

"The jury is still out on that one, guy," Wren teases, her laughter bubbling with effervescent charm. I playfully nudge her foot with mine under the table, provoking a melodramatic gasp from her.

"You poke the bear, you're going to get the claws," I counter with a smirk, a hint of playfulness infusing our banter. Waters are placed between us, and the server turns on her heels to exit.

"So you're openly admitting your feet are claws?" Wren retorts.

I cock my head to the side and laugh again, a real laugh within minutes of the other. My shoulders relax just as the cheeseburgers are placed before us. Wren lifts her bun to check for mustard, and upon eyeing the yellow devil, she smiles and places the bun down contently. She doesn't shy away from eating in front of me, biting deeply into her burger without hesitation. I follow suit, watching as her eyes light up with what can only be described as a foodie's delight. There's a reason I brought her here—they have the best cheeseburger on this side of the river. Wren holds her mouth as she chews, signaling with her eyes that it is indeed the best cheeseburger she's ever had. I smile and continue to chew as well.

The remnants of our meal linger on our plates, and I seize the moment to break the comfortable silence. "I practically lived on cheeseburgers during my college days. There was this spot near campus where they served $3 burgers, and I'd visit almost three times a day. After graduating, I couldn't stand the sight of them for years, but when I finally revisited, I tried a burger from Carl's, and it made for the best day ever."

Wren pauses, her gaze locking onto mine. "The best day of your life involved a cheeseburger, Will?" Her tone is both teasing and incredulous, a note of playful banter weaving through her words.

I'm usually meticulous about my name, preferring William over any shortened versions. Yet, with Wren, the urge to correct her dissipates, and a sense of belonging settles within me as she uses my nickname.

"Well, yeah," I respond.

"That's sad," she remarks, a simple retort that surprisingly strikes a chord within me. As reality snaps back into focus, I glance at my watch. "We have to go!" I announce abruptly, nudging us back to the present. Wren follows my gaze, a flicker of realization crossing her features as she retrieves her phone, untouched throughout our meal. I have never seen Wren without her phone in her hand unless at work.

"Time flew by! I'll flag down Kelly," Wren declares, reaching for her credit card. I halt her motion with a gentle touch, presenting a $100 bill to cover our meal. She eyes the bill on the table and stands from the booth, smoothing out her dress with her hands. She meets my gesture with a tight-lipped smile, and we make our way towards the exit. The walk back to the office continues in pleasant silence, both of us fighting a smile that desperately tries to claim our lips. The breeze carries her scent towards me, her hand brushing against mine as we walk slower than necessary.

Seventeen

Stuck With You

William

April 20th

Despite priding myself on my courage, Wren had an inexplicable power to render me weak at the knees. My attempts to focus on the budget report for the upcoming board meeting proved futile, my mind wandering as her smile plagued my thoughts. I hated that she had this effect on me. I prided myself on my control, on my ability to stay composed under pressure, but Wren had a way of dismantling all of that with just a look. Frustrated and conflicted, I turned to my email, drafting a message addressed to the board and Eric Pearson. With each keystroke, my chest tightened, beads of sweat forming on my brow. The pressure mounted, threatening to overwhelm me entirely. Just as I hovered over the send button, my phone rang, a welcome interruption to the spiraling chaos of my thoughts. Exhaling a sigh of relief, I answered the call, allowing Marcus's voice to wash over me, momentarily diverting my attention.

"Hey Will, I'm at your place and I can't find the peanut butter. Where would it be?" Marcus whispered.

"Why are you whispering?" I leaned forward, turning up the volume on my phone.

"Huh? Oh… no reason. Peanut butter. Where is it?" Marcus responded, a hint of confusion in his voice. I reached for my phone, pulling up the live feed from the kitchen camera on my home security app. There, on the screen, Marcus stood clad only in his boxers and a beanie, rummaging through the contents of my refrigerator in search of peanut butter.

"Peanut butter would be in the pantry," I sighed, shaking my head. Marcus was always so chaotic, and I couldn't help but wonder how I ended up with a friend like him— who seemed to have no concept of boundaries or logic. But maybe that was why I needed them. Marcus's carefree nature was a stark contrast to my own, and sometimes, I envied it.

"Why? It's going to get hot," Marcus exclaimed.

"Would you prefer it cold?" I asked, hiking an eyebrow although he couldn't see me. I watched as Marcus grabbed the large jar of Jif and tapped his phone, ending the call.

Glancing at the time, noticing that it was well past closing hours,

I began hastily gathering my belongings and departing from my office. The dimly lit corridors of the office building exuded an eerie tranquility, a silence I worked best in. The quiet, the order—it was where I thrived. Everything in its place, no surprises. But with Wren, there were always surprises. With each step towards the elevator, the weight of the day bore down on me, my mind racing with unanswered questions and unresolved dilemmas. It was baffling, the amount of stress that accompanied Wren's appearance in my life.

As the elevator descended into the garage, the quiet solitude of the late hour enveloped me, offering a momentary reprieve from the chaos of the day. Yet, my solitude was short-lived as the elevator abruptly halted, and a familiar figure stepped on board. My initial surprise quickly gave way to a sense of unease as I found myself standing in close proximity to Wren. I didn't need this today. With the board meeting coming and the lunch we shared, everything was scattered in my brain, the lines blurred. For a moment, we stood in silence, our eyes fixed ahead, each lost in our own thoughts. The familiar scent of vanilla and coconut lingered in the air, a reminder of her presence beside me. Vanilla aromas always informed me that Wren had recently washed her hair. I tried to ignore the way my pulse quickened, tried to ignore the way my thoughts became jumbled. I was supposed to be composed, collected—not this. Not someone whose heart raced just because of a scent.

As she turned to me with a smile, I couldn't help but feel a surge of anticipation mingled with apprehension. Her smile faltered, replaced by a look of expectation, and I found myself struggling to maintain composure under her penetrating gaze. Why did she always do this to me? It was like she knew exactly which buttons to press, exactly how to unravel me.

The tension between us escalated as unspoken words hung heavy in the air. The elevator came to a halt, and a ping from above rang loudly. The doors, however, remained closed, leaving both of us fidgeting with our personal items, awaiting their opening. I took a step forward in anticipation, but still the doors remained shut. We waited, thirty seconds in silence. In a sudden burst of frustration, Wren broke the silence, her words cutting through the stillness with sharpness.

"Were you really going to just walk away?"

"Excuse me?" I responded over my shoulder, my voice sharper than I intended. She always knew how to get under my skin.

"Oh, please, William, stop with the act." Wren rolled her eyes and huffed.

I felt the shot to my chest. "The act" she was referring to—did she see beneath it? Did she see past the flat stares and vague responses? I silently shook my head, opting not to respond. It was easier that way, to hide behind the mask. I'd spent years perfecting it—being the composed, reliable William who always had the answers. Letting someone see beyond that was terrifying.

"You're a coward," she spat, and the first thing I thought was, I know. In a feeble attempt to salvage my pride, I responded with a retort that I didn't truly mean. "You don't know anything; you're an office decorator," I said, air quotes around her title. It was petty, and I knew it, but I needed the distance. Wren's reaction was swift, her eyes narrowing to slits. As her fiery gaze met mine, I sensed a storm brewing beneath the surface. In that moment, I realized that I'd struck a nerve, triggering something deep within her. A soft spot, perhaps, hidden beneath layers of resilience and charm. The tension between us crackled, each moment fraught with the potential for conflict. I stood there, bracing myself for whatever might come, uncertain of what form her reaction would take. Would it be a verbal onslaught, or, the more worrisome, a slap?

She paced back and forth, the rhythmic sound of her footsteps echoing in the confined space of the elevator. It was as if she were engaged in a battle with herself. I watched her closely, unable to tear my eyes away, captivated by what was playing out before me. And then, abruptly, she stopped in front of me, her movements ceasing as if frozen in time. With a suddenness that caught me off guard, she extended her finger, pointing it inches from my nose. As her face neared, I saw the little vein in her forehead pulse.

"Fuck. You. Will," she stated firmly. A smirk found my mouth, and my eyes softened. The truth was, I admired her fire. I admired the way she never backed down, even when I was being an ass.

"It's William," I replied as I lowered her finger from my face.

Her brows were furrowed, creating sharp angles above her eyes, while her lips were pressed into a tight line. Her eyes, however, told a different story altogether. They darted across my face with an intensity that bordered on ferocity. As Wren released her lips from their previously flat line, I found myself unable to step away. Whenever I was near her, I became trapped in her pull, like an asteroid drawn to earth. With slow, deliberate movements, I allowed my eyes to roam over her, taking in every curve and contour with a hunger that bordered on obsession. Her breaths were slow and measured, in perfect harmony with my own, as if we were breathing in unison. I watched, mesmerized, as her chest rose and fell with each inhalation, the rhythm of her heartbeat echoing my own. And then, almost unconsciously, she licked her lips.

Unable to resist any longer, I reached out and grabbed her face, turning it towards mine with a sense of urgency that bordered on desperation. In response, she placed her hand over mine, her touch electric against my skin as she met my gaze with a mirroring desire, leaving me speechless. "You won't..." she challenged.

Still cradling her face in my palm, I leaned back slightly, studying her intently. Her expression betrayed everything I had questioned—she desired me, yearned for my touch too. If only she knew the extent of my longing, how desperately I'd yearned to taste her lips, to feel her in my arms. With a gentle touch, I lifted her chin with my finger, meeting her eyes in silent acknowledgment. Slowly, I released her, sensing her tension melting away as a small grin danced across her lips. As though she could sense the barriers crumbling between us, the walls I'd erected around my heart beginning to falter.

Leaning in, I pressed my lips softly against hers, a tender caress that ignited a spark between us. A spark that exploded instantly, morphing into a massive wildfire. Pulling back slightly, I met her eyes once more, finding reassurance in the nod of approval she offered. Emboldened, I returned to her lips with a newfound urgency, abandoning all pretense of restraint. As our kiss deepened, I felt her hands move from mine to my arms, then to my back, pulling me closer with each passing moment. With a surge of recklessness, I released her face and swiftly discarded my suit jacket, mirroring her movements as she shed her oversized cardigan, revealing the satin camisole and lace bra beneath. But as she began to unbutton my shirt, I hesitated, grasping her hands and holding them to my chest in place. My eyes silently conveyed the fear and uncertainty that gripped me, the words I was too afraid to speak aloud.

Should we do this?

It wasn't that I didn't want to. In fact, it was all I could think about—every fiber of my being dying, pleading to touch her more. But here? In this elevator? At the office? It was simply not the right time or place. I envisioned us together, alone, in the privacy of my home, exploring each other's bodies until dawn. Yet, reality intruded—the presence of Marcus, staying with me, prevented that. I was sure that Wren would not want her sister's boyfriend to be privy to our intimacy. As I considered the alternatives, like a hotel or car, doubt crept in. What were we doing? I wanted Wren, and more than just a night of heated passion. Where could this really go with her termination lingering?

"What's going on up there?" Wren whispered in my ear as she tapped the side of my temples.

"This… it's just…" I began, my voice trailing off as I placed my cheek into her palm, seeking solace in her touch. She waited patiently for me to continue, but the words eluded me, swallowed by the weight of the moment. Sensing my struggle, she took a step back, allowing me space to gather my thoughts. As I straightened, we remained locked in a silent exchange, our eyes speaking volumes as we held each other's gaze. Without breaking eye contact, Wren bent down to retrieve her cardigan from the floor, releasing a sigh, our connection unbroken even as she moved.

"I don't know what you want from me," I said, the desperation almost cracking through my resolve. I hated admitting it, hated showing vulnerability. But with Wren, it was impossible to hide. Wren took a half step, lips in a tight line, shoulders high. She didn't respond, but she also didn't look away. I tuned into her glare, searching for the response there, only to find a mirror. Every subtle shift perfectly mimicked the exact path she wanted my mind to travel. I saw past her deception—she was searching me too.

"I want nothing from you, William." She folded her arms over her chest, and then continued, "I think you are the one who needs to figure that out."

"I know exactly what I want. I always do," I stated firmly back at her, straightening my shirt for emphasis. It was a lie, of course. Wren had thrown everything I thought I knew into chaos, and I hated her for it—almost as much as I wanted her.

"Of course you do," she whispered, rolling her eyes and leaning back, trusting the elevator wall to catch her. She was so infuriating. I wanted to… I wanted to tell her she… I wanted her. A sudden noise broke the tense silence, the sound of the elevator doors opening echoing through the air. We both glanced towards the doorway and then back at each other, neither of us making a move. Finally, I tore my gaze away, grabbing my suit jacket and bag before stepping out of the elevator. I paused, expecting to hear the sound of footsteps behind me, but there was only silence. With a quickened pace, I made my way down the hallway, the elevator doors closing behind me with a finality that seemed to echo the ending of more than just this conversation.

Eighteen

Set It Right

Wren

April 27th

As I slid through the busy lunchtime crowd, weaving my way through the maze of tables and people to find the pick-up line, I couldn't shake off the feeling of being judged by Ms. Host-Stand with the superiority complex. It was common during my errands outside the office; I didn't match the aesthetic of the big rich suits in this district, so I usually received subpar service. However, today, it seemed to intensify as the particularly rude, barely eighteen-year-old host made her disdain known.

"We don't have an order for Wren. There's nothing else I can do. You can reorder it… if you want," the fire-redhead said with a twist of her neck.

"Oh my god. I spoke with Remy from to-go. My order number is 287, under Reese. Not Wren," I said again, my voice strained with exhaustion.

"I doubt it," she snickered, while scribbling something down behind the host stand. In the whirlwind of rudeness and tension, William emerged beside me, towering over both of us. "I don't believe that is how you are trained to speak with patrons, Petra."

"Oh, Mr. Jones! Hi. I didn't see you come in. Do you have a to-go order?" she asked, her tone suddenly giddy and charming. My hand itched, and I couldn't help but feel that it was a sign to smack her for her rudeness—or maybe it was the way she smiled at William.

"This here is my friend, and I am very surprised at the service I just witnessed," he stated professionally but with enough dryness to emphasize his point. He then placed his arm around my shoulders and tipped his head as if waiting. As I stood there, stunned by his seamless intervention, I couldn't help but want to melt at his tact and finesse. The smell of his cologne was intoxicating, butterflies lifting me away while the heaviness of his arm grounded me. I almost snuggled in, fitting perfectly under him like a custom-made mold, but that would break the paper-thin wall I had up against him, so I stiffened instead.

When the host finally offered an apology, her gaze remained fixed on William, almost as if she were captivated by his commanding presence. With unwavering authority, he redirected her attention, his voice carrying a weight that demanded respect. "I am not the one owed an apology, Petra," he challenged, his words cutting like a knife. Then, in a gesture that caught me off guard, he moved his arm from my shoulder and placed his hand on the small of my back, his touch gentle yet possessive. Two fingers rested delicately on the bare skin exposed between my blouse and pants, sending a shiver down my spine.

"I apologize for my behavior. I will check with the kitchen on your order," the host said as she hurried to the back. I turned to thank William, but he was already walking away, making his way back to his lair—or wherever he went on lunch. My shoulders slumped, and I exhaled the breath I'd been holding for the entire match between William and the host from hell. As I saw the said demon trotting back with a bag in hand, I jumped when an arm slid over my shoulders again. I looked up to find William towering over me, his gaze fixed forward, his arm tossed around me as if this was the norm for us.

As we made our way back to the office, opting for the stairs, the conversation drifted toward our past experiences as service workers. He didn't seem like the type who could hack it as a server—you have to have a lot of energy and a high tolerance for assholes.

"I always worked night shifts, even though the morning crowd made bank on the weekends," I said, climbing the steps one by one.

William, matching my steps, looked over with ease and said, "I loved the morning shifts. Get in there before the teenage crowds showed up."

Before I could stop myself, a laugh escaped. William paused, looking over at me.

"What?" I murmured nervously.

"That laugh," he replied, shaking his head slowly like he was savoring the sound.

"Ha! I know, I've been told I laugh really loud," I whispered as we continued climbing the steps. William gave a small, soft smile for a few moments before replacing it.

"I like it. It has character," he stated, his tone impassive, but his words ringing through me.

"Well, for your birthday, I'll gift you a record—five minutes of straight laughter. I'll even have Rick & Morty on in the background."

"Have it on my desk by five," William replied firmly.

"I said for your birthday. Wait, is today your birthday?!" I yelped. He threw a devilish smirk my way, then replied, "It is."

"What? Why didn't you say anything?" I exclaimed, pushing his arm, surprised by how solid he felt. When does this guy find time to work out?

"I just did," he retorted, pushing his glasses up his nose, and that small gesture—I wanted to stow it away in my mind forever. It was by far the only thing I could say about William that I would categorize as cute.

As we approached the stairwell exit on the ninth floor, William turned and leaned over me to open the door, catching me off guard. In a split second, my heart raced with anticipation as I leaned in, thinking he was about to kiss me. But before I could close my eyes, reality crashed down on me like a bucket of cold water—he was simply opening the door to my floor. Embarrassment flooded my cheeks as I mentally laughed at the misunderstanding, quickly regaining my composure before stepping out of the stairwell on to my floor. He turned and continued up the stairs to his floor, briefly halting on the second step but never turning back. Then the door to the stairwell shut, and I stood there blinking, speechless.

* * *

William

The workday was drawing to a close as I walked into my office, my head bowed as I scrolled through the flood of emails that had come in throughout the day. Sorting through messages was a familiar routine that helped ground me amidst the chaos of my thoughts. As I glanced up, my gaze was drawn to a small red velvet cupcake sitting on my desk. A smile tugged at the corners of my lips as I reached for the cupcake, and before I knew it, I was grinning from ear to ear.

How did Wren get in here? Why did she go through the trouble of leaving to buy me a cupcake after she'd already taken her lunch? No one else here knew about my birthday—I had made sure of that—so it had to be her. I sat down, taken aback, as my work PC illuminated with an alert from the company messenger. It was an audio file from Wren. My hands trembled as I clicked the file, and the sound of her addicting laugh filled my office. As promised, the background was accompanied by the familiar sound of Rick & Morty. I played it back on a loop five times before slumping deeper into my chair. My chest felt tight, but not in the anxious way I knew all too well. It felt like a drum beating, with all the blood in my body rushing to my ears.

What was she doing to me?

Memories of our encounter in the stairwell danced through my mind— the fleeting moment when our lips seemed to hover on the edge of a kiss. I wanted her so badly, but every move felt like the wrong one. Though I am usually reserved, I've never been scared of women—well, not since high school. I do pretty well in the dating field, when I have the time, but something about Wren takes me back to being fourteen, with pimples and knees trembling from nerves.

* * *

As the day faded into night, I found myself at a bar in a nearby town with Marcus. He insisted we indulge tonight for my birthday. Among the loud music and clinking glasses, Marcus confided in me about his plans to propose to his girlfriend, Dove. Despite his excitement, I couldn't shake my skepticism about the rushed nature of their relationship.

Marcus has always been a smooth operator when it came to women. Commitment has never been his thing, and I can relate. While our reasons for avoiding it may differ, we both stand firm in our stance. I've never seen Marcus stick around in a relationship for more than a month, and just because this current relationship has surpassed the three-month mark doesn't automatically qualify it for marriage. Yet, I was hesitant to voice my concerns, fearing Marcus might make an impulsive decision—he's always been a rebel at heart.

"You really think she's the one?" I asked, raising an eyebrow as I took a sip of my drink.

Marcus chuckled, leaning back in his chair. "Yeah, man. I know it sounds crazy, but there's something about her. She gets me in a way no one else ever has."

I nodded slowly, still unconvinced. "I mean, three months isn't a lot of time to really know someone. What makes her different?"

Marcus looked at me, his expression softening. "It's not about the time, Will. It's about how it feels. With Dove, it feels right. Like, I don't have to pretend or put on a show. I can just be myself, and she loves me for it."

I frowned, trying to wrap my head around it. "But you've always said you weren't the relationship type. What changed?"

He smiled, a genuine, almost boyish grin. "Maybe I was wrong. Maybe I just hadn't met the right person yet. Dove… she's different. She makes me want to be better. She makes me want to stick around."

I sighed, still unsure. "I just don't want you to rush into something and end up regretting it. Marriage is a big deal, Marcus."

Marcus shrugged, his eyes twinkling with determination. "I know it is. But sometimes, you just have to take a leap of faith, you know? Life's too short to play it safe all the time."

I shook my head, a small smile tugging at my lips. "I guess. Just… be sure, alright? I don't want to see you get hurt."

Marcus raised his glass, clinking it against mine. "Don't worry about me, Will. I've got this."

"And, you're sure?" I found myself asking, my curiosity piqued by Marcus's unwavering determination.

Marcus's navy eyes gazed into the distance, scanning the crowd as if searching for confirmation among the vast expanse of possibilities. It was as though every compelling reason to marry Dove was laid out before him, each one more convincing than the last. His demeanor exuded a sense of certainty, as if he couldn't fathom a single reason not to take the plunge. Before I could release the breath I'd been holding, I found myself nodding in reluctant agreement, swept up in the conviction of his beliefs.

Nineteen

Read Between The Lines

Wren

April 28th

Sitting in the basement prepping for the Mother's Day party, I go over the schedule and theme to ensure everything is just right as usual. I shoot a quick text to my sisters' group chat, hoping none of us got Mom the same gift. I opted for a gold chain with all of our initials—Mom's a sentimental soul, so I figured a tear-jerker gift would hit the mark.

Wren: Has everyone gotten Mom a gift already?

Dove: I'm wrapping mine tomorrow. Can you pick it up from Perch?

Lark: I can pick it up. I'll be down there tomorrow.

Raven: I haven't yet, but it's in my cart, ready for checkout.

Wren: In your cart??? Are you sure it'll arrive on time?

Dove: We have time.

Raven: No, I am not, but like Dove said, we have time lol.

Lark: Does anyone have a white button-up I can borrow?

Wren: nnnNO.

Raven: NO!

Dove: Sure, it'll be pressed and hanging in my office tomorrow when you pick up Mom's gift.

Wren: Lark, why are you going to be in the Business District tomorrow?

Raven: Yeah, what are YOU up to?

Lark left all of us on read.

Suddenly, my phone buzzes with a message from an unknown number. It's Marcus, Dove's boyfriend, and his words stop me in my tracks. He wants to propose to Dove next weekend and needs my help. Although his idea seems a bit out there and not exactly Dove's style, I don't question it. Excitedly, I reply, giving him my enthusiastic blessing.

Setting my phone down on the glass coffee table with iron-curved legs, I start watching the news absentmindedly. My phone vibrates again and slides off the table. As I bend down to retrieve it, something glints in the fibers of the rug—my missing earring from last June. Picking both up and checking my phone, I notice an unknown number next to Marcus' now-saved contact. Curiously, I open the message thread and discover that Marcus has added his best friend, Will, to the chat.

"Hey Wren, I added my friend Will to the chat. He's the only other person who knows, so please don't tell the rest of your sisters. Dove told me Raven and Lark are gossips, so I assumed you were the only one I could trust not to spill the beans. I need some help in the planning department, so I'm entrusting this to you and Will," it reads.

Will's response, a curt "NO," catches me off guard, eliciting a raised eyebrow from me.

Wren: Wow, okay, Will. Way to be a team player.

Will: I don't do team projects.

Wren: Too bad, because now you're stuck with me. Besides, I heard you were the best man for the job.

Will: You heard wrong.

Wren: Oh, come on. I promise not to boss you around... much.

Will: That's what they all say.

I roll my eyes at his responses, but a smile tugs at my lips. Despite his grouchy exterior, there's something endearing about his banter—a challenge that I can't help but want to rise to. Replying with an eye-roll emoji, I return my attention to the news bulletin flashing across the screen. They're warning about a possible tornado watch, but the idea seems absurd. Tornadoes hitting anywhere near Merritt City? I can't recall such an event ever happening within a 50-mile radius.

Glancing back down at the open message thread on my screen, I'm surprised to see that Will has hearted my message. Despite my efforts to maintain composure, a faint blush rises to my cheeks. To anyone else, it wouldn't be noteworthy, but I know William well enough by now to recognize that him liking my sarcastic emoji was flirting. William was flirting—under the radar, but still flirting.

Wren: Did you just "heart" my message? Are you feeling okay, Will?

Will: It was a slip. Don't let it go to your head.

Wren: Too late. Consider my head officially enlarged.

Will: Great. Just what the world needs—an even more insufferable Wren.

Wren: Insufferable? I think you mean charming. And besides, I thought you liked a little charm.

There's a pause, and I stare at the screen, waiting. A moment later, a new message appears.

Will: Don't push it, Wren.

Despite his words, I can't help but smile, my heart fluttering just a little. As we continue to banter back and forth via vague texts, I can't help but notice that Will's tone seems softer, almost friendly—well, friendly for him. Our exchange ends with Will agreeing to meet Marcus and me for brunch to discuss the proposal details. Simultaneously, excitement and dread swirl within me.

Twenty

Stay

William

April 29th

Being the first one to arrive, I take in the breathtaking ambiance of the place. It's unlike any spot I've visited before. From the outside, it gives off the impression of serving only wheatgrass smoothies, but stepping inside reveals a sleek interior. The tables are pristine white, and the orange velvet chairs, seamlessly designed without legs, provide a unique contrast.

As I settle into my seat, facing the entrance, I catch sight of Wren walking into view. She's a vision of beauty, her hair cascading down her back in straight strands, longer than I remember from her usual curls. The sunlight dances off her honey streaks, accentuating her features as she dons a white sundress peppered with small yellow dots. Upon reaching the host stand, her eyes lock onto mine, and a smile graces her lips before she can suppress it. When she reaches our table, I rise uncertainly, unsure whether to hug her, so I give a tight smile and simply gesture for her to take a seat.

She sits, and there's a single sunflower on her place setting—my little thank-you for her thoughtful birthday gift. Wren smiles and takes a deep inhale of the flower, then breaks the stem and places it behind her ear. She looks up and smiles. "Thank you," she says softly. Breathtaking, she is utterly breathtaking.

Twenty minutes drift by in comfortable silence, the tension growing between us as we swiftly down our drinks. I hadn't planned on indulging in alcohol so early in the day, but I sense I'll need the fortification for what lies ahead. Opting for a Bloody Mary, I catch a giggle from Wren before she orders a strawberry mojito for herself. I don't usually drink this god-awful thing, but I thought it would get a reaction out of her. It seems that's all I care about lately.

Our phones lay face down on the table, and as I reach for my napkin, both devices vibrate simultaneously, disrupting the tranquility of the moment. Hastily, I grab mine, only to find a text from Marcus informing us of his sudden unavailability. "Something came up," the message reads. My brows furrow in disappointment and frustration. Is this how Marcus plans to conduct himself when discussing marriage with Dove? Doubts creep into my mind, casting a shadow over the day. Glancing across the table, I notice Wren also eyeing her phone, undoubtedly receiving a similar notification. With a resigned sigh, she places her device back down, her expression mirroring my own sense of disappointment. In an attempt to distract ourselves from the unexpected turn of events, she gestures for the server to return, waving her hand in the air. The slender man, dressed impeccably in black attire, promptly appears at my side.

As the server stands by, Wren takes the initiative to tidy up our table. With practiced efficiency, she begins rearranging the used glasses, stacking them neatly to the side. Her movements are graceful and purposeful, a testament to her meticulous nature. "Can we have the check, please?" she says. The server nods and disappears again.

I find myself grappling with the idea of letting her go. The thought of her leaving hits me harder as the seconds spin by, stirring up a sense of urgency to hold onto her. "Stay," I blurt out, the word bursting forth from me like a plea.

"Why?" she retorts, her voice edged with skepticism.

"I… want you to stay," I reply, my voice barely above a whisper, avoiding the intensity of her hazel gaze as I struggle to articulate the depth of my emotions. The server's interruption jars the charged atmosphere, breaking the tension momentarily. "I'm sorry, I forgot to ask. Would you like two checks?" Wren's gaze shifts to me, her eyes searching mine for answers, as I battle to keep my crumbling walls intact, hiding the vulnerability and anxiety that threaten to spill out.

She straightens her shoulders, a surge of apprehension coursing through me as I anticipate her leaving. Each subtle movement she makes feels like another step away from me. Yet, even as I brace myself for her inevitable departure, a flicker of hope lingers within me—a desperate wish that she might choose to stay.

"My apologies, we will actually be staying. Another round," she states firmly, her words a sudden beacon of hope. In that brief moment, light cascades back into the room. I hadn't even noticed the darkness creeping from the shadows of my anxiety until she spoke.

As the lunch progresses, time slips away unnoticed during our lively conversation and laughter. The ambiance of the restaurant shifts as the dinner crowd trickles in, yet our focus remains solely on each other. With each round of drinks, our inhibitions loosen, and we find ourselves eagerly delving into an array of appetizers rather than sticking to traditional entrees. It's a refreshing change of pace, indulging in the variety and spontaneity of a smorgasbord rather than adhering to a single meal.

"So," she says, "what made you go into finance law?"

"It was a good choice," I reply without thought.

"A good fit or a good choice?" she retorts, bringing her glass to her lips, quirking her brow.

"Those are synonymous," I state firmly, crossing my arms over my chest.

"Are they, though?" she counters, meeting my intense stare.

"For me, they are," I reply. She shifts in her seat but doesn't back down, matching my stare while interrogating me.

"What about event planning? Do you feel it's a good choice, Ms. Reese?" I question with a snarky grin. Without hesitation, she replies, her eyes widening with enthusiasm.

"Good question! I'd have to say, yes. But, I don't really limit myself to event planning. I also do interior design and make my own decor most of the time." She picks at the fruit in her drink, then continues, "I'm usually very sure of the things I like or dislike. I like to create experiences, and I love parties. I've been throwing parties since I was in kindergarten. My mother literally had to beg me to stop telling other children to show up on random Saturdays. But I knew if I told her I was throwing a party, she'd say no, so I planned it and invited people. The passion was always there—just needed some... guidance."

"Wow," I stutter, almost shaken by her fierce determination and certainty.

"Yeah, well..." she murmurs, smiling as she brings her glass up to cover her mouth.

I'm struck by the genuine warmth of Wren's smile, unrestrained and radiant in the glow of the restaurant's dim lighting. It's a sight I rarely witness in the confines of the office. And to my surprise, I find myself laughing freely in her company, buoyed by her infectious joy and playful banter. It's a side of Wren I hadn't fully appreciated before.

Eventually, as the afternoon begins to fade and the air outside cools, we decide to leave the restaurant. As we step out on to the street, the vibrant hues of the setting sun cast a mesmerizing glow, illuminating Wren in a way that steals the breath from my lungs. Her face upturned, bathed in the warm, golden light, she appears utterly entranced by the spectacle unfolding above, her head pointed to the sky. Every feature seems to radiate with an almost ethereal allure, from the curve of her neck to the warm glow of her sun-kissed skin. In that moment, I'm rooted to the spot, captivated, and painfully aware that I'm spiraling out of control.

As she turns to face me, her eyes shining with an indefinable spark, I'm overcome by an undeniable surge of desire. "What is it?" she asks, her words sending shivers down my spine.

"You," I reply, the admission slipping from my lips before I can stop it. Her laughter, sweet and melodic, washes over me like a soothing balm, momentarily easing the nerves I've tried so hard to hide.

"Do you want to share a car?" Wren asks, pointing to her phone.

I actually drove here, avoiding the \$25-an-hour parking fee by parking my car two blocks away. I could've left after exiting the restaurant, but akin to a compressed spring—the further I tried to distance myself from Wren, the more intense the invisible force that yanked me back towards her became. Locked in a powerful gaze, our silence emphasized every unspoken emotion. Finally, we ordered an Uber, the city lights flickering around us as we climbed into the backseat. The mood shifted instantly, the tight quarters amplifying the tension that had been simmering between us all night. My expression remained stoic and guarded, a thin veil of restraint that I clung to tightly. Wren's eyes sparkled with curiosity, probing for any chink in my armor, and with each widening of her smile, she effortlessly dismantled my defenses. A soft chuckle escaped me, and I couldn't help but nod and smile as I crossed my arms protectively over my chest, a final barrier in place to shield myself from her undeniable entry.

The ride starts off in relative silence, both of us lost in thought, but it doesn't take long for the air between us to grow heavy with unspoken tension. A simple back-and-forth about directions turns into something more, and I never thought a simple disagreement could escalate so quickly into a full-blown argument. We're trying to help the driver navigate back on route, with construction vehicles blocking our exit, forcing us to take a detour. Of course, Wren and I couldn't agree on the way to advise the driver to go. Wren's controlling spirit matches my own, and as we clash over the smallest details, I can feel the tension mounting between us. But beneath the surface, there's something else simmering in our eyes as we argue—something I've been trying to ignore all night.

"Can't you see reason for once?" I snap, frustration seeping into my voice as Wren stubbornly refuses to back down. The car is turning left, and we both grapple to stay on our sides of the gray leather seat.

"Reason? Ha! Coming from the one who can't even admit Main Street has double the lights of MLK," she retorts, her eyes flashing with defiance. Her dress is rising to her golden upper thigh, and she pulls at the hem to lower it. I can feel my temper flaring in an attempt to mask my desire, the words tumbling from my lips before I can stop them.

"You are so damn infuriating!" I yell, loudly.

The moment the words leave my mouth, I regret them. I never yell, I never lose control. But it's too late to take them back now. Wren's expression shifts from wide-eyed anger to a shocking glimpse of hurt, and I curse myself for letting the words slip. Wren retreats further into her side of the car, as if my words had physically struck her. A crack in the wall she keeps up, the one her sparkling smile hides so well—but I see that wall. Because I too have a fortress surrounding me, eliminating anyone from getting too close.

"I… I didn't mean that," I stutter, my voice softening as I reach out to touch her arm, but she shrugs me off, her eyes filled with a familiar disappointment mixing with anger.

"Don't touch me," she snaps, her voice trembling with emotion. "I'm tired of this, of us constantly fighting. This roller coaster." I knew she would not accept my touch, but the rejection still sent needles up my left arm straight to my chest. As I watch her turn away, something inside me snaps. I can't bear the thought of losing her, not when I care about her more than I can admit or digest. And in that moment, I know I have to say something before it's too late.

"Wren, please," I call out, my voice barely above a whisper as I reach out to grab her hand. We're turning again, and the car slides us closer together. I steady myself by grabbing the headrest of the front seat. She doesn't move this time, and her soft hand slides into mine. I look down, and I feel my entire wall crumble. Every guard and fail-safe I have built instantly shatters. I intertwine my fingers with hers and I never want to let go. She clears her throat, and my eyes shoot to hers. Her eyes soften, and the brown highlights dance like she can see everything I haven't said yet.

Her hand relaxes in my secure grip. I then relax my features, pinching the bridge of my nose with my unoccupied hand. I look back to her and open my mouth. After a few beats, I say, "I… I care about you, Wren, more than I can put into words. You infuriate me because I cannot rid my mind of you! You are all I see, and when I don't, I yearn for your presence, even if it is as petty as arguing with you. I would take the scraps of you, Wren! Scraps! Like a fucking addict needing his next fix. This is not something I know how to deal with, and for the life of me, I wish I could just shut you out, but you're so entwined in my chest. I just can't…" I point to my chest, trying to pinpoint the exact spot that has become her throne. She removes her hand from mine and lays it across that spot. I look down, shock coursing through my system.

Her eyes widen in surprise, and Wren tilts her head slightly as if trying to solve me. I wait, breathless, as she continues to lean toward me. The energy between us hums with newfound intensity. Before I can second-guess myself, I close the distance between us, my lips meeting hers in a passionate, desperate kiss.

The world falls away, leaving only the two of us, lost in the heat of the moment. I grab the side of her face, and she stretches her neck to grant me more access. She returns my kiss with such fervor—she's a fever dream I never want to wake from. Wren's lips part, and I do something I never do—I nip her bottom lip, desperate to see if she's real. There's a whisper of a moan that escapes her, and I pull back, looking at her. My eyes dance over her features—she's emanating lust and desire, swollen lips and heated eyes—my fantasy come true.

Twenty-One

Entwined

Wren

April 29th

As we stumble through the door of William's house, our shoes kicked off in a hazy blur, I can't help but take in the sight of his impeccably decorated mini mansion. Every corner is adorned with taste and style. My inner decorator is slightly envious, and I can't help but mentally note the way the colors and textures work so well together. But my attention is quickly drawn elsewhere as William's lips find their way to my neck, igniting a trail of shivers down my spine and drawing a low, involuntary moan from me. With a daring glint in my eyes, I hike my leg up around his waist, pulling us closer as our lips meld in a fiery kiss.

Effortlessly, he lifts me, and a gleeful, almost girlish laugh escapes my lips as he carries me up the stairs. I love how strong he is; it makes me feel weightless, carefree. He lays me gently on the large, firm bed, his movements filled with a potent mixture of power and reverence. As he tears open his shirt, buttons scattering like confetti, I find myself admiring the sculpted perfection of his physique—a god among mortals. His chocolate-brown skin is covered in tattoos across his chest and upper arms. William has tattoos? A lot of them. All I can think is how much I want to run my fingers over every single one.

But before I can even begin to undress myself, he stops me with a commanding yet tender gaze, laying me back down with a slow, deliberate touch. My skin burns with desire. With each piece of clothing he removes, his lips follow, tracing a path of heated kisses along my skin, leaving me breathless and yearning for more.

"You're so fucking beautiful," he murmurs huskily once I'm left in nothing but a white strapless push-up bra and blue lace thong. His words send a thrill coursing through me, igniting a fire that burns hotter with each passing moment. I want him inside me now.

As he sheds his pants, revealing the undeniable evidence tenting his black boxer briefs, I feel a surge of anticipation course through me. His smirk only adds to the intensity of the moment. With a sudden burst of energy, I leap off the bed, surprising him with my boldness, pulling him down with me. His expression flickers with surprise before giving way to hunger. As he falls back onto the bed, I straddle him, reveling in the power and passion that courses between us, ready to lose myself in our intoxicating dance. Will's grip on my hair is firm, commanding, pulling me closer until our breaths mingle, hot and heavy. "Mine," he asserts with a quick, firm tug before claiming my lips in a searing kiss that leaves me dizzy with need.

Our bodies move in perfect harmony, a symphony of passion and lust as I grind against him, the friction driving us both to the edge of insanity. With each thrust, each movement, the barrier between us thins, until there's nothing but want coursing through our veins. The sharp sting of his hand against my bottom sends a rush of adrenaline through me, a mix of pain and pleasure that only heightens my arousal. Another smack, harder this time, and I can't help but moan in response, the sensation fueling the fire between us.

As my thong is torn away, I gasp at his strength—he's so in control, so confident. Now, only his boxer briefs separate us, the barrier driving us both to the brink of madness. With practiced ease, he frees me from my bra, exposing me fully to his hungry gaze. I arch into his touch, my body humming with anticipation as he lavishes attention on my breasts. His hardness presses against my core, a promise of what's to come, and I can't resist the urge to grind against him harder, seeking more of the delicious friction.

In a brief moment of responsibility, I ask, "Do you have protection? I'm on the pill, but, ya know." He opens his side drawer. The cherry oak nightstand is small, and the drawer only contains a notepad, pen, a remote, and an empty condom box.

"Fuck! Mark must've taken from my stash." Frustration flickers across his face, and his hands fall from my hips, but I refuse to let this moment slip away. With fierce determination, I intensify my movements, urging him on with a silent plea. His hushed moans of pleasure spur me on, his touch finding my thighs. In one swift motion, I guide him inside me, the sensation of just his tip filling me with an immense shock of pleasure. William throws his head back in ecstasy and mumbles, "FUCK, Wre…" as I continue to slide down his length.

His touch is like fire against my skin, his lips trailing kisses along my neck and chest as he takes me to new heights of ecstasy. The heat rises to a fever pitch, anticipation coiling tighter with each deliberate thrust. His movements become languid, sending waves of pleasure cascading through me as he leans up, grabbing my hair to bring my face to his. His brown eyes lock onto mine with a hunger that ignites every nerve. As his lips meet mine in a fiery kiss, he claims me as his own with a possessive growl. "Mine," he breathes against my lips, and I surrender to the overwhelming ecstasy coursing through me. As our bodies move as one, I realize that this moment, this connection, is unlike anything I've ever experienced before.

* * *

Waking up alone in his large bed, I stretch out, feeling the emptiness beside me. The room is dimly lit by brown and cherry curtains, keeping the morning light at bay. There's only one painting hanging on the wall, opposite the bed where a TV would normally be. I notice a remote on his nightstand, which strikes me as odd since he doesn't have a TV. Then a more pressing question flares—where is Will?

Realizing it's only early morning, I get up, feeling the soreness from our passionate frenzy last night. We went four times after our initial session. Stumbling towards the bathroom inside his room, I catch sight of myself in the mirror, startled by the disheveled reflection staring back at me. My mascara is smudged, giving me raccoon eyes, and my hair is a tangled mess. "Oh, great, I look like I've been through a wind tunnel," I mutter to myself with a mix of amusement and exasperation. I waste no time and step into the shower, instantly feeling the warm water wash over me. I use Will's conditioner to finger-detangle my curls and his soap, relishing the lavender scent that now envelops me, reminiscent of him.

Stepping out of the mist-filled bathroom, I grab the t-shirt lying on the chest at the end of his bed. Pulling it on, I inhale deeply, taking in more of his scent. "Mmm, cozy," I murmur, feeling a bit more like myself. Opening his bedroom door, I'm greeted by the sight of a long hallway and a grand staircase leading to the living room. I hear panting before I see his dog charging towards me. He has a slight limp on his left side, but he looks old, so I figure it's normal. I pet Jerry Smith and give him a good morning hug. "Where is your dad?" I say as his wide eyes look at me adoringly.

I make my way downstairs, silently admiring the beauty of his home. From the outside, it may appear unassuming, but inside, it's stunning. The archways, the antique knobs on the doors, and the elegant eggshell-colored walls complement the ash carpets perfectly. *I could get used to this*, I think to myself, mentally picturing what my own place could look like someday—if I ever manage to save enough.

Downstairs, the aroma of bacon and pancakes fills the air, drawing me to the kitchen where I find William shirtless, flipping pancakes on the griddle. He must be expecting company, as there's already two plates full next to him. *Pancakes and abs? Okay, this man is trying to ruin me*, I think, smirking to myself. It's Saturday, thankfully, so I can make my exit without an awkward encounter at work.

Sneaking back upstairs, I locate my clothing and get dressed. William ripped my underwear, so I leave those behind. *R.I.P. cute blue lace, you will be missed,* I mutter with a small smile. Heading back downstairs, I head for the red front door, opening it and stepping outside silently only to realize I have no idea where I am. I'll need to request a car. As I prepare to step off the porch, I hesitate, opening my contact list in my phone and typing a text to William, only to erase it three times. *Come on, Wren, just say something casual,* I scold myself under my breath. Just as I'm about to make my first step off his property, the door opens behind me, and there stands William, leaning against the frame.

Caught off guard, I struggle to find an excuse, but words fail me. "Escaping already, huh?" he says, crossing his arms over his exposed chest. His muscles are flexing, more prominent in the daylight, and his tattoos look glorious. There's tribal art across his torso and what looks like anime characters his biceps. The one that holds my attention most is the long, realistic samurai sword that lines his collarbone, shoulder to shoulder.

"Stay," he demands, and my will weakens. He uncrosses his arms and extends his hand. I look down at it and then back to him. *I don't know what I'm doing, but maybe that's okay,* I think to myself. Unsure of everything now that the night is over, I take his hand reluctantly and step back inside, feeling the uncertainty gnaw at me.

"Are you having company?" I inquire as he closes the door behind me, raising an eyebrow and trying to sound casual. *Don't let him see how nervous you are, Wren,* I remind myself.

"No, not that I know of. Mark is with Dove for the weekend," he replies, his words sending my thoughts into a tailspin. My sister dating his best friend and us working together adds so much to the current emotional turmoil swirling in me. *Why does everything have to be so complicated?* I think, biting my lower lip. I knew these things before going into whatever this is, or what happened last night, but now, in the light of day, they seem more difficult to brush over. Sensing my hesitations, William takes my hand again, his touch grounding me. He looks at me with a newfound sense of calm and assurance, a stark contrast to the previous William I've gotten to know. "How does he make everything seem okay?" I wonder, cracking a smile, leaving my worries behind as he pulls me into his embrace. I meet his chest, and I hear the hum of his heart, feel the contours of his toned physique. His arms around me—a promise, an answer, an invitation.

"I made you breakfast. I didn't know what flavor you liked best... so I made them all," he whispers against my neck, and I realize the abundance of pancakes was his way of trying to please me. I smile and pull him in tighter. *Well, he definitely knows the way to my heart*, I think, feeling a warmth spread through me.

After we eat, we spend the day watching movies, playing with Jerry Smith, and listening to podcasts while we cook or play cards, lost in each other's company. "This is almost too perfect," I muse, trying not to overthink it. That night, the comfort of his presence feels like a slow burn rather than a roaring fire. William's touch is deliberate, his movements tender but restrained, as though he wants to communicate something he can't yet say aloud. When morning comes, I wake to find his arm still draped over me, a rare moment of vulnerability in his usually composed demeanor. *I could really get used to this*, I think, smiling softly.

* * *

When morning breaks, I stir to the sound of William's dog whimpering beside the bed. Concerned, I glance at the animal, noticing a lethargy in his eyes that wasn't there before. Instinctively, I reach out to pet him, but he flinches away, his discomfort evident. "Uh-oh, what's wrong, buddy?" I say, my worry growing.

"Something's not right," I murmur, my voice laced with worry. I shake Will to wake him up. William murmurs and turns in bed, then he hears the whimpering, and his eyes shoot open. His brows angle as he watches Jerry Smith waddle to his side of the bed. Without a word, we both jump up and agree to take him to the vet.

At the clinic, the atmosphere is tense as we wait for the vet's diagnosis. Time seems to crawl agonizingly slowly, torturing any hope remaining. The office is small and white all over, except for the painted paws on the floor leading to the exam rooms. I'm wearing William's gray sweatpants and white t-shirt since I have yet to return home. "We probably look like a hot mess," I think, glancing at our reflection in the clinic window. He's sitting next to me in matching attire, gloom written all over his face.

Finally, the vet emerges, her expression grave. She guides us to the last exam room in the hall, and once she closes the door behind us, I feel my stomach knot. "Please let it be something treatable," I think desperately. I look over to Will and grab his hand instinctively. Once our fingers are laced together, he seems to alleviate just an ounce of worry.

"I'm so sorry to inform you," she begins, her voice gentle but sorrowful. "Jerry Smith has late-stage lymphoma." The words hit us like a sledgehammer, shattering the fragile hope we held onto. *Oh no... I think,* my heart sinking. William's grip on my hand tightens in the midst of the devastating news, but his face remains stoic. Together, we listen as the vet outlines the treatment options, but it's clear that the prognosis is grim, the timing worse.

As we leave the clinic, the weight of reality settles upon us, casting a shadow over our once carefree weekend. William's eyes are clouded with sorrow, and I ache to ease his pain, to offer him some semblance of comfort in this dark hour. *How do I even help with this?* I think, feeling helpless. I lean over and rub his shoulder nearest to me, words lost, and he shoots me a small smile. But I see the pain in his eyes.

"Tell me what to do, Will," I say in my most serious tone. He turns to me, eyes defeated.

"I… I don't know," he replies, his voice smaller than usual, but still smooth and deep. *And that scares me,* I think, but I don't say it out loud.

Back at his house, we sit in his living room in silence, grappling with the enormity of what lies ahead. It's in this moment of vulnerability that I feel the need to give him something. So I say the first thing that comes to mind.

"I'm terrified of failing," I confess, my voice barely above a whisper. "Starting my own business feels like leaping into the unknown, and the thought of not succeeding… it paralyzes me." William listens intently, his gaze softening with empathy.

"I understand," he murmurs, his tone leveled. "But you're capable of so much more than you realize. And no matter what happens, you'll succeed. I know it."

In turn, William opens up about his own struggles, revealing a fear that's long haunted him. "I've been hurt before," he admits, his voice tinged with vulnerability. "And the thought of opening myself up to that again… it terrifies me." I inch closer to him and rest my hand on his knee.

I reach for his hand, offering him the same comfort he bestowed upon me. "Love is a risk," I concede with a wisdom I do not apply to my own life. "But it's also the greatest adventure life has to offer. You just have to be sure—sure the person is worth the fall. That they'll catch you." I look him in the eye to drive my point home. He returns the warmth, but there's something more lingering, hiding. *I hope I'm worth the fall,* I think, but I keep that part to myself. Our conversation is interrupted by the buzzing of my phone, signaling a message from Dove. As I read the text, a crease forms between my brows, and his expression becomes inquisitive.

"Mark's acting weird," I mutter, using air quotes, remembering the entire reason we met up was to plan Dove's proposal. "I should go check on her. Dove's a little flighty. If she senses trouble with Marcus, she'll run." William nods in understanding, recognizing the importance of saving Marcus and Dove's relationship. With a lingering glance, I rise from my seat, preparing to leave. But before I go, I turn to William, meeting his gaze with a mix of uncertainty.

"Okay," he says softly, his eyes heavy with unspoken emotions.

"I can come back," I say, and he smiles.

"Wren, it's fine. Go help your sister." He rises from the couch and places a kiss on my exposed shoulder since I now have my sundress back on. I give him a quick hug and head out.

As I step outside, the morning sun warms my skin, but the weight of what just happened still lingers. My phone buzzes again, and I see Dove's message lighting up the screen. I know this day is far from over. Taking a deep breath, I start walking, my mind already racing with thoughts of what Dove might need and what waits for me back at William's. With a final glance at the front door, I head towards my next chapter.

Twenty-Two

Loss

William

May 1st

The emptiness in the house echoes louder than ever, a constant reminder of the absence of my best friend. Jerry Smith is gone. I chose to avoid a painful end and had him put to sleep "peacefully." My chest feels hollow, my mind dark and chaotic. I've had Jerry Smith since I graduated college, back when we were crammed into a tiny studio apartment, surviving on nothing but Ramen noodles for me and clearance kibble for him, and, of course, each other's company.

The silence is deafening, and the memories of our time together flood my mind, each one a painful reminder of what I've lost. I find myself sinking deeper into sadness, grappling with the harsh reality of loneliness. Every step I take, every breath I draw, is haunted by the weight of his absence. I regret every moment I denied him a throw when I was busy, or the late nights at the office that kept him waiting.

Each minute, I retreat further into the recesses of my mind. Emotions are hard for me to process; they don't always make logical sense, and without reason or logic, I find it impossible to analyze them. I'm not proud of this. It's why I hesitate to date with any serious intentions—to keep the inevitable disaster from happening when a woman demands more, more access to a place I myself have yet to visit.

My silence is not by choice but by necessity, a shield I wield against the pain of human connection or the misunderstanding of it. But amidst the darkness, there is a glimmer of light. Wren. She appeared in my life like a shooting star, offering comfort and warmth in my darkest hour. With her by my side, I felt a sense of solace that I hadn't experienced in years. She sat with me in my pain, understood my silence, and, most of all, I wanted her to be there.

Now, as I sit alone in the quiet of my home, her presence lingers in my thoughts. I want to reach out, to thank her for everything she's done, but the words elude me. How do you express gratitude for something so profound, so life-changing? Then what happens after that? Where do we go from there? So much unknown territory accompanies Wren's entrance into my life.

I pick up my phone, my fingers hovering over the screen, but uncertainty holds me back. What do I say? How do I push past the pain to talk to her? What happens when we return to work? **The board meeting**! The pain in my chest doubles. This is too much; my mind feels scattered, torn. In the end, I settle for silence. With so much emotion bubbling within me, I'm overwhelmed. I need to step back.

* * *

Wren

I managed to quell Dove's suspicions about Marcus, and for now, they seem to be on good terms. However, Marcus better act fast with his plans because Dove won't stick around if things start feeling off. Dove's compassionate and affectionate nature contrasts with her aloof demeanor, which I attribute to her being a classic I-don't-need-anyone Aquarius. Marcus explained that he postponed his proposal due to William's recent loss of Jerry Smith, wanting to include him in the celebration once he's ready to move forward from his grief. I sent William a text when I heard the news, but he never responded, which I expected—William is definitely the sulking type.

Arriving at work the following day, I took the elevator up to the 12th floor, hoping to catch sight of Will, but his dark office and closed door extinguished my hopes and multiplied my worries. William has never missed work—at least not in the time I have been employed here.

I sent two text messages to him when I got home at the end of the day, but once again, he didn't respond. I then sent a meme the next morning, and again, no response. I understand that he's hurting, but he can't just ghost me after the magical weekend we shared, minus the visit to the vet. At this point, the ball is in his court, whenever he's ready to join the game.

I can't help but reminisce about that weekend—the way his laughter filled the room, as if all his worries were momentarily forgotten. It was a side of William I hadn't seen before, one that was relaxed and carefree. We spent hours watching old movies and cooking way too much food together, and the effortless comfort between us felt like something out of a dream. I want to be there for him now, but it hurts feeling so shut out. I want to help carry some of his pain, to let him know he's not alone, but every unanswered text feels like another wall he's putting up between us. I know he needs his space to heal, but I can't shake the feeling of helplessness, like I'm standing on the other side of a locked door, desperately wishing he'd let me in.

Even with the uncertainty, I can't shake the feeling that William and I have something real. It's rare to find someone who can make you feel both challenged and completely at ease, and despite the current radio silence, I believe in us. I'm hoping that when he's ready to open up, I'll still be here, but I won't wait for long. He has to know that I'm not going to stand still forever, waiting for him to let me in, again.

Twenty-Three

Turning Point

Wren

May 4th

As I hit send on the email blast for the upcoming Mother's Day bash, a surge of excitement coursed through me. It was going to be a fantastic event, and I hoped everyone would enjoy it as much as I had planned. However, my moment of triumph was interrupted by the ping of a new email notification. Curious, I opened it to find a message from Eric.

"Hey there, fancy seeing you in my inbox," the email read. "Care to swing by my office for a quick chat?"

The invitation caught me off guard. Eric was known for his sense of humor and laid-back demeanor, but it wasn't often that he reached out to me personally. Nevertheless, I decided to seize the opportunity and headed over to his office.

As I entered, Eric greeted me with a warm smile. "Hey, glad you could come up. Have a seat," he said, gesturing to the chair opposite his desk.

"Thanks, Eric. What's up?" I asked, settling into the chair.

Eric leaned back in his seat, a mischievous twinkle in his eyes. "Well, I couldn't help but notice your email about the Mother's Day bash. Sounds like it's going to be fun."

I chuckled, relieved that the conversation wasn't going to be about anything serious. I'd half expected it to be a termination meeting. "Yeah, I'm really looking forward to it. It should be a fun celebration for all the mothers in the office."

"Only mothers are invited? I am crushed," Eric said, playfully clutching his chest.

"Well, you're welcome to push a basketball-sized child out of a ping pong-sized exit," I replied with a smirk.

"Ouch," he said, wincing, and I laughed.

We chatted for a while, discussing plans for the event and sharing a few laughs along the way. But then, out of nowhere, Eric rose from his chair and walked around his desk. He sat on the edge of the desk, opposite my chair, the light from his large window shining perfectly on his back, illuminating his dark gray suit and broad shoulders. We both stared at each other, the silence deafening. His brown eyes were soft, and while they resembled the brown of William's, they held none of the depth. He leaned in, and I moved back cautiously. He then leaned further and whispered, "You know, you are so, so beautiful, Wren." Eric gently lifted my chin to meet his eyes as he spoke.

I smiled nervously and tucked a stray hair behind my ear, avoiding his gaze. Confused, I blinked in surprise. "Uh, Eric, what was that for?" I stammered, feeling a flush rise to my cheeks.

Eric's expression turned sheepish, and he scratched the back of his neck awkwardly. "Sorry about that. I don't know what came over me. I guess I just got caught up in the moment. I... I like you, Wren. You're fun to be around. You remind me of someone."

I couldn't help but grin at his flustered demeanor. He was the epitome of confidence, with his impeccable physique and perfectly tailored suits, and it was rare to see him lose his composure like this. Yet, beneath his charming facade, I sensed a vulnerability that tugged at my heartstrings. It was totally inappropriate, but at this point, I'm used to men being attracted to my light. But I know all too well how, when they capture it, they only desire to keep it in a cage. "It's okay, no harm done," I reassured him, swiping nonexistent lint off my lap, my voice laced with a hint of nervousness.

A wave of unease washed over me, leaving behind a sharp pang of anxiety in my chest. Thoughts of William flooded my mind, his image looming large despite our undefined relationship. Even though Eric and I were just colleagues, being in such close proximity to him in this situation felt like tiptoeing on a moral boundary, and guilt gnawed at the edges of my conscience. I... should leave.

Suddenly, Eric's face grew serious, like he could see my mental gears spinning anxiously, and he reached out to grasp my hand but hesitated, hovering a few inches away. "Listen, please don't say anything to HR about this. I know it was completely out of line, and I regret it already."

Surprised by his earnest plea, I found myself nodding in agreement. "Of course, Eric. I won't say anything. Nothing happened," I confirmed, hoping to ease his obvious distress. Relief flooded Eric's features, and he pulled me into a grateful hug. "Thank you. I really appreciate it," he murmured, his voice filled with gratitude.

A deafening clang echoed through the air, the sound slicing through the tense silence like a blade. My heart plummeted as I turned to see William standing there, his hand forcibly pushing the door open as if it were made of paper. The sudden commotion drew the attention of everyone on the floor, their eyes fixated on the unfolding scene before them. In that moment, the air felt charged with an ominous energy, thick with anticipation and dread. Meeting William's gaze, I was met with a sight that sent a chill down my spine. His normally warm eyes were now dark pools of fury, his expression tight with barely contained rage. As he strode purposefully toward us, each step seemed to reverberate through the room, amplifying the growing tension. Panic tightened its grip around my chest, suffocating me with its chilling claws.

"I-It's not what it looks like, Will," I stammered, my voice trembling with nerves.

William held up his hand, silencing me with a single gesture. "Nope," he growled, his voice low and menacing, his eyes focused on Eric.

Eric, sensing the escalating situation, attempted to diffuse the mounting tension with a casual remark. "William, to what do I owe the pleasure?" But William ignored him, his focus now entirely on me. With every advancing step, he seemed to grow larger, more imposing, casting a towering shadow over us. The fear that gripped me was throttling, an immeasurable weight pressing down on my chest, making it difficult to breathe. In that moment, the office felt like a war zone, and I was caught in the crossfire, paralyzed by the threat of William's wrath.

As William approached Eric, the tension in the room amplified further. I could practically hear the unspoken accusations crackling between them. Eric stood his ground, but there was an undeniable stiffness to his posture, a subtle acknowledgment of the power dynamic at play. In contrast, William's demeanor radiated a potent mix of fury and disdain, his towering figure casting a shadow that seemed to swallow Eric whole. It was as if he was channeling the wrath of ancient gods, his eyes ablaze with a fire that could incinerate everything in its path. His silence only added to the ominous energy brewing. With each step he took, the floor seemed to tremble beneath his feet. As William reached Eric's side, the energy in the room shifted, crackling with an intensity that sent shivers down my spine. I stood frozen, caught between the two opposing forces, feeling like a mere pawn in a high-stakes game of chess.

Without uttering a single word, William's actions spoke volumes. I began backing up, uncomfortable with the power play at hand, and then William grabbed my hand. His grip was both reassuring and possessive. It was as if he was staking his claim, marking me as his own in front of his perceived adversary. Still, not a word left his mouth, not even a grunt of disapproval. As he guided me out of Eric's office, I trailed behind, my hand still in his grip. The eyes of the office followed our every move, their stares like daggers piercing through the thin veneer of composure I tried so desperately to maintain. Each glance felt like a judgment, a silent condemnation of the chaos unfolding before them.

With each passing moment, my mind raced, a whirlwind of conflicting emotions swirling within me. Fear, uncertainty, and a tinge of excitement mingled together, creating a turbulent storm inside me. Should I speak up, try to diffuse the tension? Or should I remain silent, allowing him to process what he thought he saw? As we waited for the elevator, the silence between us stretched taut, my heart pounding in my chest, the rhythm erratic and unsteady. In that moment, I felt utterly exposed, laid bare before William in a way that left me vulnerable and raw. His eyes were dark, and his breaths were even but heavy. And as the elevator doors finally slid open, I couldn't help but wonder if this was just the beginning of a storm that would tear apart everything we've built.

Twenty-Four

Let Go

Wren

May 10th

As Mother's Day approached, my sisters and I embarked on our annual tradition of planning a luncheon for our mom and aunts in the backyard. Although we did this every year, we continued to plan in secrecy. The sun beat down relentlessly, casting a sweltering heat over us as we busied ourselves with decorating. Despite the cheerful atmosphere, a lingering sadness gnawed at me from within—a constant reminder of the man that clouded my thoughts.

As I stepped inside to tie my hair up, I couldn't shake the feeling of unease that gripped me. It had been days since I'd heard from Will, and the radio silence only fueled my anxiety further. Gazing at my reflection in the mirror in my bedroom, my eyes drifted to the note I had received on my birthday, tucked away in a corner of the frame. The familiar handwriting never failed to bring a smile to my face, a brief respite from the turmoil brewing within me. Clutching onto that small token of affection, I drew strength from its comforting presence—a beacon of light in my darkness. I didn't know why I clung to this damn note, but it felt special.

Just as I stepped out the back sliding door, Dove arrived, her vibrant energy filling the yard. She was absolutely glowing. Lark and I exchanged looks, and Dove tamed her wide smile for a moment while she rolled her eyes.

"Hey, Dove! You made it," I said while putting the pile of leaves Raven raked earlier into a trash bag.

"Sorry I'm a bit late, traffic was insane," Dove said, sitting in the lawn chair next to us.

"No worries, Ray was here earlier. You can help with setting up the table, though," Lark replied. "By the way, you look amazing!" she exclaimed, stepping back to admire Dove's newfound glow.

Dove blushed. "Thanks! So, guess what?" Silence followed for a few beats while Lark and I raised our brows, waiting for the news we knew was coming.

"Marcus proposed last night!" she yelped, then pulled her left hand out of her dress pocket to show off the gorgeous ring. It was a white gold band gleaming in the sun, with a three-stone setting, sparkling with a trillion-shaped diamond nestled in the middle. This ring screamed

Dove. I couldn't have picked out a better one for her myself. It shows how much your man knows you by the ring he picks out, and I could say Marcus was off to a phenomenal start.

"Oh my gosh, that's incredible! Congrats, Dovey!" I screamed.

"What?! Oh my god. Let me see the ring!" Lark yelped, rushing towards Dove to see her ring in the light.

Dove held out her hand further, her smile the brightest I had ever seen. She wore happiness well. She wasn't even this ecstatic the first time she was proposed to. "Isn't it beautiful? I can't stop staring at it!" Dove exclaimed.

"Wow, Marcus did a great job," Lark said, placing one hand on her hip and eyeing Dove.

"Seriously, you both look so happy. I can't wait. When's the wedding?" I asked.

"Oh, I have no clue! He just proposed last night in bed. I'm so happy he didn't do some elaborate public proposal. It was perfect," Dove said, smiling as if mentally reliving the night.

Lark grabbed the bag out of my hand and threw it to the ground. "Well, let's celebrate! We've got a lot of the prep for the luncheon done. It's day-drinking time," she said in a singsong voice. "I'm going to text Raven to get her little butt back here." I giggled as we headed inside.

Dove's announcement of her engagement brought a burst of excitement, momentarily overshadowing my own worries. Yet, as we sat in the kitchen waiting for Raven to return to join us, my mind couldn't help but drift back to Will. How could he just go mute on me like that? I mean, I get having sex and ghosting me, but having me be your dying dog support system and then ghosting me is baffling.

Amidst the chaos of drinking and Dove telling us the proposal story over and over, a delivery arrived—a small Amazon box addressed to me. I tore it open to reveal a bracelet, engraved with the name "Rick." The realization hit me like a ton of bricks—this was meant for Will, a reminder of our inside joke. I'd ordered it the morning after we had that earth-shattering sex. Anger surged within me, mingling with the frustration and confusion that had been building up inside me for days.

Throwing the bracelet to the floor, I felt a surge of emotion threatening to overwhelm me. My sisters all eyed the bracelet and then me. I didn't want to explain whatever I had with William, so I just laughed and said, "They sent me the wrong damn bracelet." They all nodded like they'd experienced Amazon's faulty shipping and returned to the reality show we were watching. It had been so long since I had allowed myself to feel anything this intensely, the floodgates of pent-up emotion threatening to burst open. But I refused to let the tears fall, swallowing back the lump in my throat as I grappled with the roller coaster of emotions that William had unwittingly set into motion. I didn't even know why I would cry over him. We had sex—phenomenal, back-breaking sex—but still just sex. This was not going to become some slow-burn romance, and I needed to get that through my thick skull.

As the day drew to a close, I left my sisters downstairs and returned to my room with the excuse of work. As I lay on my bed, opening emails and scrolling mindlessly through threads, I halted, phone almost dropping from my hand. There was an email from HR from yesterday.

Taking a deep breath, I clicked on the thumbnail and read through the entirety of the long, professionally toned message.

They fired me.

Twenty-Five

The Great Assist

William

May 15th

Sitting in my living room, surrounded by the echoes of Marcus's joyous engagement news, I can't help but feel a heavy weight settle in my chest. Marcus is beaming, his excitement palpable, but I can't find it in me to fully share in his elation. Instead, I'm consumed by a storm of conflicting emotions, each one more tumultuous than the last.

"Can you believe it, Will? I'm going to be a married man!" Marcus exclaims, his grin infectious as he gestures to the sparkling ring on his fiancée's finger in the photo he's showing me. His enthusiasm fills the room, but it only serves to highlight the hollow ache gnawing at my insides. I miss my dog, and I miss Wren, yet I'm frozen with indecision on how to move forward with her. That weekend, we skipped so many steps, and my mind is in loops trying to straighten out our timeline and what makes sense.

I nod, offering a tight-lipped smile, my mind elsewhere. "Yeah, it's great. I'm proud of you, man. I really like Dove for you," I reply, my tone lacking the enthusiasm that Marcus radiates. I try to push aside my own turmoil, focusing instead on being happy for my friend, but the effort falls short. I know I should be more excited for Marcus, but everything feels muted, like I'm watching my life through a foggy window.

Marcus chuckles, nudging me playfully. "Come on, Will, you look like you just lost your goldfish. Don't tell me you're still moping about that office incident?" His teasing tone is gentle, but it cuts through me nonetheless, exposing the raw nerves beneath the surface. I stiffen at the mention of it, the memory of seeing Eric too close to Wren still fresh in my mind.

I shrug, trying to keep my voice casual. "It's nothing," I mutter, my voice clipped. I can feel my jaw tightening, a habit I haven't been able to shake since I was a kid. It always happens when I'm trying not to feel things too deeply. But Marcus isn't one to let things go easily. He leans in closer, his expression earnest. "Seriously, man, if something's bothering you, you can talk to me about it. You know that, right?" He leans back in the loveseat across from me and crosses his leg over his knee.

I meet his gaze, seeing the genuine concern in his eyes. I sigh, my shoulders slumping slightly. Despite my usual inclination to keep my feelings to myself, I find myself opening up to him. "It's just...

complicated," I admit, my words weighed down by all the feelings I can't verbalize. I try to articulate the jumble of emotions threatening to overwhelm me, but they remain tangled, just out of reach. I hate not having control over my own thoughts—it's like trying to solve a puzzle where all the pieces are the same color.

Marcus nods, his understanding evident. "Love always is, my friend." His words strike a chord within me.

"Love?" I huff, my brow furrowing. I can't help the skeptical scoff that escapes me. Love is messy, unpredictable, and I've always prided myself on being the guy who thinks things through, who doesn't leap without looking. Love feels like the opposite of that—chaotic, vulnerable.

"Yeah, L-O-V-E," he repeats while swiveling in the loveseat like a child. His carefree demeanor makes me envy him. How can he be so sure, so fearless?

"I don't…" Marcus cuts me off before I can finish my foolish statement.

"Come on, man, be honest with yourself. You love her."

Shocked by his observation, I ask, "Love who?" I told Marcus about Wren and our weekend, but what did he gather from that to categorize it as love?

"Will, you spent an entire weekend with Wren. You love your alone time and hate people in your space, and I'm just going to guess she didn't hold you at gunpoint to make you do those things," he says, rolling his eyes.

I frown, rubbing the back of my neck. "Yeah…" I reply, working through the rapid thoughts in my head. He's right. I value my space, my routines, the comfort of solitude. But with Wren, it was different. It wasn't an invasion; it was… comfortable. I hate admitting that Marcus might be right, but there's a kernel of truth in what he's saying. The realization makes my stomach flip—like that moment before a big drop on a roller coaster.

Marcus leans forward, resting his elbows on his knees. "Look, Will, I've known you for years. You're a logical guy. You like structure, predictability. And that's fine. But when it comes to Wren, I've seen a different side of you. You're more… open. You're willing to bend your routines for her. You're not just tolerating her in your space—you want her there. That says a lot more than you realize."

I stare at Marcus, trying to process his words. "I mean… I don't know if I'm ready for all that," I admit, my voice hesitant. "It's not like I planned any of this. I didn't expect her to mean so much to me."

Marcus nods, a small smile playing on his lips. "That's the thing about love, Will. It doesn't wait for you to be ready. It just shows up, turns everything upside down, and you have to figure it out as you go. Trust me, I didn't plan on falling for Dove either, but here we are. You just have to decide if she's worth the risk."

I let out a shaky breath. "But what if I'm wrong? What if I tell her, and it messes everything up? What if she doesn't feel the same way?" My voice cracks slightly, betraying the fear I've been trying so hard to hide.

Marcus leans back, his gaze softening. "That's the risk, man. But look at it this way—if you don't tell her, you'll never know. You'll always wonder 'what if.' And I've seen the way she looks at you too. There's something there, Will. You'd be a fool not to at least try."

I shake my head, a small smile forming despite the anxiety gnawing at me. "You're really pushing for this, huh?"

Marcus laughs, a deep, hearty sound that fills the room. "Of course I am. You deserve to be happy, Will. And I think Wren makes you happy, even if you're too stubborn to admit it."

I let out a reluctant chuckle. "Yeah, maybe. But you know me—I like things to be neat, to make sense. This… this is anything but that."

Marcus grins, his eyes twinkling. "That's the beauty of it, my friend. Love isn't neat. It's messy, unpredictable, and sometimes it doesn't make any sense at all. But that's what makes it worth it. You can't solve it like one of your equations, but you can feel your way through it. And if anyone can figure out a way to make it work, it's you."

I look down, the weight of his words settling over me. Part of me wants to argue, to say that I'm not ready, that it's too risky. But another part—the part that remembers Wren's smile, the way she laughs, the way she makes everything feel just a little bit brighter—can't help but wonder if Marcus is right.

"Just think about it, Will," Marcus says, his voice gentle now. "Don't over analyze it to death. Sometimes you just have to take a leap. And I'll be here, whether you fall or fly."

I meet his eyes, the sincerity there almost overwhelming. I nod slowly. "Yeah… I'll think about it." It's not a commitment, not yet, but it's more than I could have said before this conversation. And maybe, just maybe, it's a start.

Marcus smiles, leaning back into the love seat with a satisfied expression. "That's all I ask, man. Now, can we please talk about something less emotionally exhausting? Like, I don't know, how you're going to be my best man?"

I let out a laugh, shaking my head. "Best man, huh? Are you sure you want a guy who overthinks everything standing next to you?"

Marcus grins. "Absolutely. Who else is going to make sure everything runs perfectly? Plus, I need someone to keep me in line."

I roll my eyes, but the warmth in my chest is undeniable. "Alright, alright. I'll do it. But don't blame me if I give a speech full of law jokes."

Marcus laughs. "Deal. Just make sure Dove doesn't fall asleep during it."

We both chuckle, and for the first time in a while, I feel a sense of calm settle over me. Maybe things aren't as clear-cut as I'd like them to be.

* * *

Wren

As Lark meticulously weaves my hair into small cornrows, the soft hum of the fan she's using to dry her lash glue and the gentle rustle of her movements fill the air, creating a comforting rhythm that soothes my restless thoughts, despite the kink in my neck from the way she's pulling on my hair. I sit at my laptop, surrounded by the warm glow of the screen, scanning through endless job listings in a seemingly bottomless sea of opportunities and rejections.

With each click of the trackpad, frustration gnaws at me, fueled by the lingering bitterness of recent events. The memory of that day with Will in the office burns ferociously in my mind, casting a shadow over my usual pleasant demeanor. Did he truly orchestrate my termination, or was it merely a coincidence that I was fired within days of him finding Eric and me talking? If he wasn't behind me getting fired, then why hasn't he reached out? Clear his name, anything! After the beautiful night we had, the things we shared, and his dog… it was just all too much for him to disregard me like I was nothing. Anger and uncertainty battle within me, and I slam my laptop shut, sliding the white device to the floor beside me.

"I swear!" I mutter, my voice tinged with frustration.

Lark's hands pause for a moment, then continue, her fingers deftly threading through the end of my hair with practiced ease. "Don't worry, Wrenny. The perfect opportunity will come along when you least expect it, just like before," she reassures me, her voice laced with confidence.

I nod, trying to take comfort in her words, but the nagging doubts persist. I'm almost 30; I can't keep repeating this cycle of jump, fly, fall, repeat.

As I continue my dark spiral, a different idea begins to take root—a seed of possibility that blossoms into a daring vision. Why wait for someone else to offer me a chance when I can create my own destiny? My shoulders straighten as Lark ties the ends of my hair with a little black band.

"I could open my own business, like officially officially," I muse aloud, the words tumbling from my lips before I can stop them.

Lark's eyes widen with excitement, her face alight with enthusiasm. "Well, duh, Wren! You have the talent and the eye. I can help you, but it will cost ya!" She quips, landing a playful pluck on my freshly braided scalp.

"I won't be able to pay you for quite a while," I say, laughing off her suggestion.

"Your money is no good here. I will take payment in other forms." Lark says devilishly, rubbing her hands together.

I turn my head to face her. "What on earth are you talking about?"

"Oh, nothing… I'll help though. So count me in," she replies, turning my head at an unnatural angle to capture a candid shot to post on her hair service page—which also doubles as a tarot reading page and a knitted beanie page.

Encouraged by her unwavering support, I feel a surge of newfound confidence coursing through my veins. Yes, starting a business is risky, but hey, no risk, no reward, right?

But even as I contemplate the possibilities, thoughts of Will linger at the back of my mind like stubborn ghosts, refusing to be banished. I shake my head, trying to push them aside, but they persist, taunting me.

"Why haven't you made a move towards Will?" Lark's voice breaks through my reverie, pulling me back to the present with her telepathic statement.

I sigh heavily, feeling the weight of the unspoken truth pressing down on me like a leaden cloak. Leaning back onto the wall of the bathroom behind me, I find myself opening up to her in a way I haven't since high school. With each word, I peel back the layers of my roller coaster of a relationship with Will.

"The standoffs, the weekend at his place, the heated encounter in the office…" I recount each moment with a mixture of anguish and resignation, the memories swirling around me like a tempestuous storm. "I thought I understood what was happening between us, but now I'm not so sure. I think he played me, and the crazy thing is… I never saw it coming."

Lark listens intently, her expression a mix of concern and empathy as she absorbs my words. With each passing moment, I feel a sense of relief wash over me, as if unburdening myself of this secret has lifted a weight from my shoulders.

"It's just… I don't know what to do anymore," I admit, my voice trembling with uncertainty. "I thought I had it all figured out, but now everything feels so… complicated. Not just with him, with life! Like he brought a whole storm with him and turned my life upside down."

Silence trickles in as Lark nods her head with understanding beyond her years. She reminds me of my mother when she's in this state. It's funny because I always compare her to Grandmother Willow from the Disney movie Pocahontas—so attuned, like an all-knowing spirit only loaned to us for this short lifetime.

"He just ghosted me!" I yelp, my voice momentarily cracking.

Lark reaches out, her hand finding mine in a comforting gesture of solidarity. "Sounds like a lot of pride and ego," she reassures me, her voice gentle yet firm while she rubs circles on my back.

"You think he's being prideful?" I ask, looking up at her.

"I think YOU are," she says, eyeing me with a look I can't decipher.

"What do you mean? Where has my pride gotten in the way?" I retort, offended, standing and wiping my legs free of the stray hairs.

"Have you reached out to him? Asked him why he reacted that way? Didn't his damn dog die?" Lark throws my way while leaving the bathroom.

"No, well yes, well… Listen, I texted him! Like five times!" I yell, following after her.

"You don't usually let men in, and when you do, you overanalyze everything to stay two steps ahead and remain in control the whole time. I don't think Will is someone that can be predicted as well as you originally thought…" Lark throws behind her back towards me while jogging down the steps.

"Hey! You're supposed to be on my side!" I reply, and she halts at the bottom of the steps, turning dramatically slow towards me.

She gives me a look—a look that tells me I need to get out of my own way. I drop my scowl and nod, understanding, but the doubts still linger like stubborn lint balls on your best cardigan. Despite my best efforts to rationalize my feelings, I can't shake the nagging sense of confusion that gnaws at me still.

"I just wish I knew what he was thinking," I confess, my words tinged with frustration. "Does he even care about me, or am I just fooling myself?"

Lark's gaze softens. "I can't answer that for you, Wren," she says gently. "But what I do know is that you deserve someone who values you for who you are, flaws and all. Someone who doesn't run from you but to you… William also deserves those things."

"Flaws?" I squeak, pitching a brow at Lark. She laughs in reply and continues to the kitchen.

Her words strike a chord deep within me, resonating with a truth that I've been reluctant to acknowledge. I realize that perhaps the answers I seek lie not in Will's actions, but in my own heart.

Twenty-Six

Brick By Brick

Wren

June 27th

I had already begun planning Eric's birthday party before I lost my job, so I brought my sisters along to avoid any awkward encounters with him or other employees from the firm. Dove, dressed in a blue long dress with a sweetheart neckline, and Raven in a fitted black cocktail dress, were deep in wedding planning mode. They sat at a table in the corner, their heads bent together over their phones as they organized every last detail. Lark, wearing bell-bottom jeans and a cream knit one-shoulder crop top, was dancing with the property litigation assistants.

I perfected Eric's idea for his party, transforming the space into a vision of sophistication and elegance, with hues of blue and silver lining every corner. My signature touch—the soft glow of twinkling fairy lights—draped across the ceiling, casting a magical ambiance. I wanted people to feel like they had stepped into a dream, an ethereal escape from the usual corporate parties.

Tables covered in crisp white linens were accented with shimmering silver touches. The centerpiece of each table featured stunning arrangements of blue blooms nestled amongst silver foliage, adding a touch of natural beauty to the sleek, refined decor. At the center of it all stood the circular bar, a beacon of indigo, where expert mixologists crafted exquisite cocktails named after Eric's favorite things. Yes, I had to ask the man who had a hand in my termination what his favorite things were.

The sound of clinking glasses and lively chatter filled the room as I circulated through the party. I felt like a fish out of water among the faces of my former colleagues, but I held my head high, shielding myself with a smile. My smile was my armor, my way of pushing through discomfort. If I was going to be here, I might as well look like I owned the room. The whispers and sidelong glances only served to confirm my status as the "fired girl with her hand in both cookie jars." Which wasn't even close to true. I had nothing going on with Eric. Okay, maybe there was some innocent flirting, and before William stormed out of the office with his hand locked around my arm, the office had assumed William and I hated each other.

As I stood at the back of the party, my eyes eagerly scanned the crowd, and I caught sight of Will entering the room, an hour later than everyone else, as if my thoughts had summoned him. With each step, the crowd around him parted, drawing my focus like a bull to a red flag. Hopefully, there wasn't steam blowing out of my nostrils.

I tried to ignore the way my heart skipped a beat at the sight of him. He was dressed in a perfectly tailored blue suit, every line and contour of his body accentuated flawlessly. An air of confidence and sophistication wrapped around him like a cage I once thought was his throne. The deep navy blue of his jacket complemented his chocolate skin tone, while the crisp white shirt beneath added a touch of classic elegance. Yet, I saw past the expensive armor he used to hide behind. While my smile had always been my weapon, Will's weapon of choice was status—I saw it so clearly now.

My thoughts halted when I realized where we were. Eric's birthday party. I was 1000% sure William would not attend. He hated Eric. It had been a while since the office incident, but I couldn't imagine they'd become buddies.

As he caught my eye from across the room, a small smirk played at the corners of his lips, sending a shiver down my spine. Was he happy to see me? If so, why hadn't he reached out to see me one-on-one? Maybe it was a polite smile, but Will wasn't polite for company's sake. I quickly looked away, focusing my attention on the DJ as I walked over to instruct him on when to announce the speeches.

I knew I had to keep my composure. No way was I going to let him rattle me. Rule #1: If someone makes you feel small, make them feel smaller, then smile bigger. And I did, plastering on a grin that I knew masked the turmoil inside.

Throughout the night, the party unfolded smoothly, with Eric even going so far as to publicly commend my efforts in planning the event.

It was a small validation, but it buoyed my spirits nonetheless. When someone asked for my business card, I proudly handed it over, grateful for the opportunity to showcase my growing entrepreneurial success.

As the evening drew to a close and the speeches concluded, I decided to steal a moment of respite on the veranda. Stepping through the white French doors, I was immediately embraced by the gentle caress of the cool night air, a welcome relief from the heat of the bustling party inside.

Leaning against the stone balcony railing, I gazed out at the expansive night sky stretched out before me. Above, a canvas of deep midnight blue was dotted with a myriad of sparkling stars, their twinkling lights forming constellations that seemed to tell stories of their own. I loved the stars. I couldn't name one if my life depended on it, but that wasn't the point of the stars. They weren't left to us to label; they were stories found within the soul, each unique to its viewer. Where one person could see a cat sipping tea on a log, another could see Italy in the fall.

I chuckled softly to myself, remembering how as a kid, I'd always try to make up stories about the stars. I'd tell Lark and Raven the wildest tales, insisting that the sky held secrets only I could decipher. I guess part of me still felt that way, the magic and wonder of it all still lingering.

A gentle breeze rustled through the leaves of the nearby trees, carrying with it the scent of freshly cut grass and the faint hint of floral perfume from the garden below. The rhythmic chirping of crickets provided a soothing background melody, further enhancing the sense of serenity. As I closed my eyes and tilted my face upwards, I felt a sense of calm wash over me, the worries and stresses of the day melting away in the embrace of the night. In that moment, I allowed myself to be fully present, to breathe.

When I turned to find a seat, my gaze fell upon Will, seated quietly alone in a chair, his eyes fixed on me with a searching intensity. A rush of conflicting emotions washed over me as I struggled to find the words I longed to say. Instead, I made a hasty retreat, rushing through the doors and weaving my way through the crowd on the dance floor until I reached my sisters' table. I wasn't ready for whatever collision with William the universe constantly threw at me at the worst timing.

"It's time to go," I announced, my voice steady despite the whirlpool of emotions swirling inside me. With a final glance back at the balcony doors to make sure he wasn't following me, I led my sisters out the side entrance, leaving behind the echoes of laughter and music as we stepped outside.

My sisters all shared a knowing look. "What?" I asked, attempting to avoid eye contact with all three of them.

Lark, taming her stray hairs, leaned into the circle and whispered, "It's time we tell her about the letters." Raven cut her eyes to me and then to Dove. Dove lifted her head from the circle, her faux ponytail swaying to each side before settling back around her shoulders. If Dove was going high, there was definitely a low coming.

"What letter?" I asked, placing my fists on my hips. They all turned to face me—three versus one.

"What… letters?" I repeated, annoyed.

"William. He gave Marcus some letters… to give to Dove, to give to you," Lark murmured, shifting from one foot to the other, rubbing the back of her neck with just a hint of nerves.

I turned to Raven, and she was scratching her elbow—yup, she felt guilty.

"When did he give you these letters, Dove?" I said, turning to the one seemingly undisturbed by the conversation rolling out.

"Oh, just a few days ago. I told Lark, and then Ray, and well, we hadn't decided whether to give it to you or not," Dove said, shrugging.

"Oh…kay. Well, I don't want them," I said, crossing my arms over my chest indignantly.

They all stared back at me, and then our valets arrived. I was riding with Dove, luckily, so I avoided dealing with Lark and Raven's probing questions.

The car was silent. Dove was the only person I knew who drove to nothing. No music, no podcast, no nature sounds—nothing. I think that either makes her the most enlightened person ever or a psychopath. To be honest, it's 50/50.

"I don't want the letters, Dove," I blurted out. She remained silent, yet subtly nodded in a way that meant she heard me and respected my decision. I pulled at the seatbelt and aimed for the radio before Dove swatted my hand away.

"I will not give you the letters, but I will keep them. If at any point I feel you need to read them, I will give it to you," she said calmly.

"Why would I need to read them?" I asked, rolling my eyes. Once again, she nodded in reply. After a beat, I knew she wouldn't further the conversation, so I sat back in my seat and watched the cars pass by.

And maybe, just maybe, a part of me wondered what William had to say. But I'd never admit it.

* * *

William

Tonight, she wore a red silk wrap dress that clung to her curves like a lover's embrace, the slit on one side teasing glimpses of her toned legs with each step she took. Her golden skin glowed under the soft lights of the balcony, radiating a warmth I wanted to drink up like hot cocoa on a cold day. I still hadn't received a response to my letter, so I could only assume she was over me—a realization that felt like a dagger to the chest.

As she entered the balcony, her hair swept up in an elegant updo with loose curls cascading down her neck, I was entranced by her. I truly could not control myself when Wren was near. I'd have traded a year of my life to kiss a trail down her long neck; make it ten years, and still I'd die a happy man. I had been waiting out here, watching the night sky above, hoping for a chance encounter with her. And as if by some tragic desperation, here she was.

Standing before me in all her resplendent glory, I couldn't help but feel a surge of emotion welling up inside me. It was as if time stood still with her, and all I could think about was how much I had missed her, how much I had screwed up. I didn't mean to "ghost" her, as Ayla put it, but it was just too much, too soon. What had started as a risky weekend became an avalanche of emotion and connection. With losing Jerry Smith, Marcus returning, his engagement, my feelings for Wren overwhelming my senses—I lost it. It was too much change, too many unforeseen futures and decisions. I needed time to step back and analyze, the only comfort I knew to hold onto. But how could I explain that to a woman who now looked at me as if I were the dirt beneath her shoe?

I had even called a truce with Eric just to be here tonight, knowing she wouldn't miss the party. It wasn't easy, swallowing my pride to make peace with the one person I thought I'd never reconcile with. But it was worth it if it meant catching even a glimpse of her.

Her eyes were on the stars, and mine traced her body like it was the last chance I'd have. I wanted more; I could almost feel her touch on my skin, her hair scattered across my chest. Wren turned, her face filled with bliss and contentment until I fell into view. Her eyes dropped, her smile became a tight line, and the light surrounding her darkened instantly.

In that moment, the weight of our unspoken history hung heavy in the air. There was a palpable tension between us, thick with unspoken words and unresolved emotions. As I looked deeper into her eyes, searching for the Wren who was once wrapped in my sheets, I could sense the distance, the chill that wasn't there before. She had been building, brick by brick, that wall that kept me out before.

Every line etched into her face told a story of hurt and disappointment, and I couldn't help but feel a pang of guilt deep in my chest. I knew that I was the architect of this estrangement, the one who allowed my own insecurities to drive a wedge between us. And now, faced with the consequences of my actions, I was left grappling with the regret of what could have been. I never intended to hurt Wren, but as I ran from my own grief and insecurities, I ran from her as well. It seemed her initial assumption was right: I was a coward.

The ache in my chest intensified as I realized the magnitude of my mistake. How could I have let someone as incredible as her slip through my fingers? How could I have been so blind to the depth of my feelings until it was too late? As she turned to leave, I steeled myself with resolve, knowing that I couldn't undo the past, but I could certainly fight for a chance at a future.

Twenty-Seven

4th of July

Wren

July 4th

As I worked the last-minute Fourth of July gig I had booked, a sense of nostalgia washed over me. Back home, my family was gathering for our annual cookout, a tradition we had upheld for as long as I could remember. I couldn't help but feel a pang of longing for their company. But as I glanced around at the bustling event, surrounded by laughter and music, I was reminded of why I was there. My business was flourishing, and for that, I was grateful. It was a testament to my resilience and determination—a silver lining in the stormy clouds that followed after Pearson, Williams, & Malek fired me. At the time, it had felt like the end of the world, but looking back, I realized it was the push I needed to take a leap of faith and pursue my dreams. While I would have rather been at home enjoying the cookout, this was the sacrifice they talked about when it came to becoming an entrepreneur. One day, I would have a staff, and I wouldn't miss events—just like Dove.

As I stepped onto the scene, the vibrant colors of red, white, and blue greeted me at every turn. The sound of laughter and chatter filled the air, mingling with the upbeat melodies of patriotic songs playing in the background. I checked the visuals from afar to make sure they matched the exact idea my client had described to me: simple, patriotic, and chic.

My client's backyard had been transformed into a sea of festivity, with tables draped in striped tablecloths and centerpieces of miniature American flags. The scent of grilled burgers and hot dogs wafted through the air, tempting my taste buds and stirring up memories of childhood cookouts.

Children darted around the yard, their faces painted with stars and stripes, while adults gathered in small groups, engaged in conversation, sipping on ice-cold beverages to beat the summer heat. The sun hung low in the sky, casting a warm golden glow over the event as guests gathered eagerly around the barbecue grill, awaiting the first batch of perfectly charred burgers and juicy grilled corn on the cob from the hired grill master.

As dusk fell, the party took on a magical quality, illuminated by the soft glow of twinkling string lights and the flickering flames of sparklers. The night sky came alive with bursts of color as fireworks exploded overhead, painting dazzling patterns against the velvety black canvas. As the show unfolded before me, I wondered what was happening over at my parents' house right then. My heart ached with FOMO, and I almost pulled out my phone, but I stopped myself. I had to be professional—I was on the job.

This Fourth of July party, a kind gesture to help out a previous client in need, felt like a cruel twist of fate. While everyone celebrated, I couldn't shake the feeling of heartache that gnawed at me from within. It was supposed to be a distraction, a way to forget about missing my family's cookout, but instead, it only amplified the ache in my chest. Dove had informed me that William would be attending my family's cookout along with Marcus, so I made sure I'd be busy. Every laugh and smile around me felt like a twist of the dagger embedded in my heart. William had ruined so much for me, and now, on one of my favorite holidays, I was thinking of him even though I went to great lengths to avoid him.

The way he had looked at me at Eric's party, after disappearing from my life, was the nail in the coffin. Exhausted by this toxic dance, I had to leave, because if I had stayed even a moment longer, I would have completely let everything I built to keep him out shatter. It all felt like a cruel joke now, written by some wannabe romance novelist. Seeing him on my birthday, working for his firm, even down to the last-minute dinner date—how could I have been so blind? The man was a walking pool of emotional unavailability, and I jumped right in, never checking for a life raft.

He had just left me hanging—no response to my texts in the days after the office incident. No email, nothing. Cold turkey, like I was some terrible habit he needed to quit. The truth hit me like a ton of self-deprecating bricks: I was nothing more than a pawn in his game, a disposable object to be used and discarded at his whim. He had probably concocted this whole thing just to fire me anyway, and yet, as I thought that through, I sadly found myself defending him against my own allegations. What the hell was wrong with me? He. Did. Not. Want. Me.

* * *

William

Accompanying Mark to Dove's parents' Fourth of July cookout felt like stepping into a bittersweet reunion. The warm summer air was thick with the scent of barbecue and the sound of laughter, mingling with the lively hum of conversation. Red, white, and blue decorations were posted all over the space, from festive banners fluttering in the breeze to patriotic tablecloths draped over picnic tables laden with trays of grilled meats and bowls of colorful salads.

As I stepped onto the spacious backyard deck, I was greeted by the inviting aroma of sizzling burgers and the tantalizing sight of rows of cold alcoholic drinks chilling in ice-filled coolers. The crackle of fireworks in the distance added to the festive ambiance, casting colorful bursts of light across the night sky. Scanning the crowd, my eyes searched for her, but she was nowhere to be found, and a pang of disappointment washed over me, mingling with the anxiety that churned in my gut. Instead, my gaze fell upon Eric, a figure I never expected to see in this setting. What stunned me even more was the sight of Eric's hand intertwined with Lark's, their laughter ringing out like a melody against the backdrop of the party. The sight sent a jolt of shock through me, but I pushed it aside and exhaled. This wasn't about Eric—it was about finding Wren, about confronting the feelings that had haunted me since our last encounter. I even brought the bundle of letters I'd been writing to her in secret. She hadn't replied to my first few, but I had a feeling that a few of these might provoke a response, at least.

As the evening unfolded and the festivities continued, I couldn't shake the nagging sense of unease that gnawed at the edges of my mind. The laughter and chatter of the partygoers seemed to blur into the background as I continuously searched for her, my heart racing with each passing family member who resembled her. Just when I began to fear that she wouldn't show, her cousin Lorraine mentioned that Wren couldn't make it because of a client commitment. Relief washed over me, mingling with a pang of disappointment. If she had a job, maybe she wasn't avoiding me—just busy with work. I'd told Dove to inform Wren I was coming; I didn't want to cause more tension by attending unwelcome.

As the evening wore on and the sky gradually darkened, casting a blanket of shadows over the gathering, couples around me nestled closer together, their laughter and affectionate gestures serving as a painful reminder of what I now longed for with Wren. In that moment, among the flickering glow of the fireworks on the horizon, I made a silent vow to myself. I would no longer allow fear of vulnerability or uncertainty to hold me back. I couldn't keep hiding behind walls of silence and logic forever. In that moment, I knew that I was willing to risk it all for just a chance with Wren.

Twenty-Eight

Love Letters

Wren

July 7th

I'm jolted awake by a sudden double-knock at my bedroom door. It's midday, but last night passed without a single ounce of rest. My heart races as I sit up in bed, my gaze darting towards the door just in time to catch a glimpse of a thin bundle of letters being slid onto my floor. The door shuts swiftly, followed by the sound of hurried footsteps retreating down the hall. Curiosity and apprehension flood my mind as I scramble off the bed, hastily tugging on my shorts before rushing to retrieve the stack.

Sitting cross-legged on the floor, I face my closet and carefully remove the red ribbon holding the letters together, my hands trembling slightly with anticipation. I pull a Jiffy Lube receipt out of the first envelope. I place the receipt down, confusion washing over me. Opening the other envelopes, my confusion only grows. All of them are filled with notes scribbled on the most random things: napkins from the bistro in the office building, the Jiffy Lube receipt, a note on a Chinese takeout menu beneath the daily special. One envelope even contains a cookie fortune that wasn't written on, but the generic message read: "A great life is awaiting you."

The last letter holds a full sheet of paper, and I begin with that one. The same small sentence—the one I've carried with me since my birthday:

Wren,
What a light you are...
William

I continue reading, my breath catching with each note:

Wren,
The more I try to avoid you, the more you're thrown in my path,
and the more I cannot deny I am tethered to you, loyal to you,
like a man to his country.*
William

Wren,
I dream of you dancing, in the diner on Carlyle, in that red dress,
and each time I wake, I dread the inevitable run-in where I'm
forced to pretend you aren't the literal woman of my dreams.
William

Wren,
I've always found it difficult to express what's in my head, but that doesn't mean I don't feel it. I write these notes to relieve my mind of you, yet as I continue to write them, I am granted no relief. I don't know what to make of that.*
William

Wren,
I want to hold you, I want to kiss you, I want to... so much with you it burns a hole in my chest.
Will

Wren,
I am so sorry for my behavior in Eric's office. I saw him close in on you and lost it. I couldn't think for the first time—I was all reaction, no thought. I have never been unable to control a situation, and losing my resolve scared the hell out of me. I found out you were let go, and I fought for you to be rehired—I put my own position on the line—but the board denied my multiple requests. Without any solution, I couldn't reach out to you, not with the entire situation being my fault. I never meant for any of this to happen.
Will

Wren,
I want to make things right, but the more time that passes, the more I feel it's too late.

William

Wren,
I miss your laugh, your smile, and most of all, you in my arms.
Will

Wren,
Tonight, I watched you watch the stars. I don't know where I'm going with this... I miss you.
Will

Wren,
Let's talk when you're ready.
Rick

As I read the notes, my heart pounds in my chest, and my mind races with a whirlwind of emotions. I never expected this from William—such raw, unfiltered thoughts. He let me in, in the only way he knew how. I sit there smiling down at the bundle of notes, an overwhelming spark growing in my chest. Without thinking, with a surge of determination, I leap to my feet, hastily tucking the small bundle of letters into the pocket of my pajama shorts before darting downstairs.

Bounding down the stairwell and into the living room, I catch sight of Dove and Lark peeking out from the kitchen walkway, their expressions a mix of surprise and curiosity. It dawns on me that they must have been involved in orchestrating this. Without wasting another moment, I snatch my mother's car keys from the hook by the door and dash outside. Thankfully, William's place is only a short ten-minute drive from my parents' house, and with adrenaline coursing through my veins, I waste no time starting the engine and racing towards his house.

As I navigate the familiar streets leading to William's place, my hands clench the steering wheel tightly, despite the sweat making them slick. With each beat of my heart, it feels like a drum pounding in my chest, the intensity of my emotions threatening to drown me. Just one block away from his house, I can't bear to waste another second in traffic. Parking the car hastily, I practically leap out of the driver's seat and begin sprinting towards his house. Every step feels like an eternity as my mind races with a torrent of thoughts and feelings, propelling me forward with a sense of urgency that borders on desperation. Time blurs as I focus solely on reaching him, my heart driving me relentlessly towards whatever awaited me at his doorstep.

As I ascend the steps to his front door, my breath comes in ragged gasps. I feel a whirlwind of nerves swirling within me. I pause, realizing I hadn't formulated a plan for what I would do when I arrived. I had acted on impulse, propelled by an overwhelming desire to see him. Doubts creep in, threatening to paralyze me as I question the wisdom of my impromptu visit. Turning away from the door, I find myself face to face with William, who stands frozen in surprise, a grocery bag slipping from his grasp, its contents scattering across the ground. Without a moment's hesitation, I kneel to gather the spilled items, my hands trembling as I grasp the half-gallon of milk.

As I rise to my feet, our eyes meet. His expression is a mix of shock, confusion, and something else I can't quite decipher. Summoning a smirk, I speak the words that hang between us like a fragile thread. "I got your letters."

He nods, still processing my arrival, and then, like a shot of smooth dark liquor, his warm voice breaks through the silence. "Must've been a mix-up at the post office," he quips, barely dawning a grin.

I smile, and his gaze heats. William closes the gap between us, his lips meeting mine with an intensity that ignites a fire within me. I surrender to the passion of the moment, letting go of everything as our bodies intertwine. My shoulders relax, and my arms become liquid around him. His strong hands grip my waist, lifting me as if I weigh nothing, and I wrap my legs around him, clinging to him as if he were my lifeline. In that moment, nothing else matters but the connection between us, the unspoken longing that had lingered between us for too long.

As we stand there, lost in each other's embrace, our lips speak volumes that our words never could. It's a love story hidden beneath layers of silence and pride, a tale of longing and desire finally unleashed. He moves towards the door and unlocks it in record time. With each step, his hands grow more primal, and as the door clicks shut behind us, I know there's no turning back. The anticipation crackles in the air as he ascends the stairs, his back taut with muscles under my fingertips. I nuzzle into the lines of his neck, inhaling cedarwood and amber. Nipping at his ear, his pace quickens with every step.

He bulldozes through his bedroom door, tossing me onto the bed with a hunger that leaves me breathless. His eyes burn with desire as they rake over me, the fabric of my pajamas suddenly feeling stifling against my skin.

"Did you wear that here?" he murmurs, his voice low and husky, gesturing to my clothing as we enter the room.

I glance down, suddenly self-conscious in my pajamas—a cut-off yellow crop top and shorts. "Um, yeah," I stammer, feeling a flush creeping up my neck.

He halts my attempt to remove my shirt with a firm grasp of my arm. "You don't wear that here and get to wear it home, nah-uh," he declares, wagging a finger towards me. Raising an eyebrow at his playful admonishment, I watch as he approaches with predatory intent. My legs part instinctively, and he settles between them, his gaze smoldering with desire. With a single grip, he tears my shirt from my body, leaving me exposed and vulnerable before him. My breath catches in my throat as his gaze lingers on my bare chest. With a predatory grace, he closes the distance between us, his hands exploring every curve of my body with an urgency that sends fireworks through me.

I've never felt anything like this—a craving that burns and consumes—but as we come together, I know this is right.

Twenty-Nine

Epilogue

Four years later...

I feel a kiss on my exposed shoulder, and I squirm under the comforter. Another kiss, and then another. The light peeking in through the window tells me it's at least 7:30 in the morning—time to start the day. I hear footsteps getting closer, then silence. A beat passes, and I relax back into a comfortable snuggle with my pillow. A rush of cool air tickles my exposed skin, and I burrow further into my warm oasis. Just five more minutes.

The comforter is suddenly ripped away, and I push myself up on my elbows, giving my husband a death stare. He's smiling at me with that devilish grin I love to hate and hate to love. I wriggle in the lingering warmth of the sheets and stick my tongue out at him.

"Had to let the light in the room, my love," he says with that smooth, sinful voice while rounding the end of our bed. I smile, glancing at the closed curtains, knowing he meant me. He sets a mug on the bedside table. Decaf tea with oat milk—my new signature drink.

"How are my girls doing this morning?" he asks, kissing my forehead before moving lower to plant a kiss on my swollen belly.

I smile and lift his head, bringing his face to mine. Wary of morning breath, I keep his face just inches away. Without hesitation, he closes the distance, kissing me like it's the very first time. His hair is longer these days, long enough for me to give it a nice tug when I'm feeling playful—which, thanks to hormones, is almost every day now. Except for the first four months. Back then, I didn't even want to look at him, let alone touch him. Dr. Nwobu said that was normal, and luckily, we're over that hump. Though I definitely thought I'd end up on a true crime documentary after the way he sliced my sandwich one day.

"We're good. Only three bathroom breaks last night," I say, forcing a smile. Sitting up and swinging my legs off the bed, I exhale deeply, already exhausted for the day.

"You know you can wake me up, my love. I'll keep you company," he says, laughing as he pulls off my one remaining sock. I roll my eyes playfully and give him a gentle shove. He offers his hands to help me up, and I take advantage of the assistance, waddling to my feet.

"I am not waking you up just to sit with me while I pee," I huff as I waddle toward the master bathroom. He's right behind me, hands on my hips, giving me support. I take two more steps when I feel a huge gush of water splashing down my legs and feet. I freeze, looking down, then stare at the bathroom ahead of me.

"Did I just pee myself?" I ask, genuinely concerned for my bladder.

"Uh, I think that's your water. They said in Parent 101 it would look like that," he replies, calm and cool.

"That can't be my water. I haven't felt any contrac—" I wince, bending over and grabbing my lower belly. "What the fuuuu—" I yell. There's no way this is happening. I knew a baby would eventually have to come out of there, but not today!

"Okay, okay, it's time. Let's go. The bag is packed and in the car, the doc is on speed dial, we can call on the way—" He's pacing now, listing everything off as the pain doubles by the minute. I watch him pace, mentally checking off his list, the contractions slowly subsiding. Braxton Hicks is very common—I've had quite a few scares in the past few weeks—that's all this is. I start to smile, even chuckle. This isn't real.

And almost as if my unborn child herself decided to test my humor, I feel the most painful stabbing sensation stretch from my back to my lower belly.

"Let's goooo!" I howl. He grabs me, guiding me down the stairs, grabbing the car keys and two hoodies from the hooks by the door.

The drive is twenty minutes, and in those long, excruciating minutes, I regret yelling earlier. Those earlier pains were nothing compared to these. It feels like I'm being stabbed repeatedly in my stomach, and just as the pain wavers, the knife twists and drags to my back before starting all over again. I'm not sure I can do this. I'm forgetting to breathe, my mind unable to settle on a single thought. The pain is overwhelming—I feel it everywhere, like tiny needles.

"We're here!" he says, throwing the car in park. A nurse standing outside the Labor & Delivery unit rushes to my door, opening it. An orderly follows behind her with a wheelchair. They both assist me into the chair and begin rolling me inside.

"Wai—my… husband!" I yell, waving my hand to stop them. "I'm right here, my love," I hear from behind me, and I feel his hand on my shoulder. My nerves relax for just a moment—until the next contraction.

* * *

After what felt like an eternity of labor, our little bundle of joy, Summer, finally arrived.

I was completely drained after hours of pushing and an unexpected C-section, but the exhaustion melted away the moment I held our daughter in my arms. She was perfect—a tiny replica of Will, with his rich chocolate skin, big brown eyes, and that adorable button nose. He says she has my "fiestiness," and I couldn't think of a better trait to pass down to her.

As I lay there, taking in the sight of my beautiful baby girl, I couldn't help but steal glances at Will. He hadn't left my side, not for a single moment. Our car was probably towed, but I knew he'd miraculously have that handled too. Sitting in the rocking chair, cradling Summer as if she were the most precious thing in the world, his eyes were filled with so much love and tenderness that it brought tears to my eyes.

I've seen Will soften over the years, especially after our wedding two years ago, but this was a whole new level—a new version of him unlocked. It felt like I'd found the prize at the end of a tricky level. He was shining so brightly, his love illuminating me, and I couldn't help but think… *What a light you are.*